Routledge Revivals

Socialism and Modern Thought

Originally published in 1895, this title provides fascinating insights into the development of socialism in the decades prior to the explosion of 20th century socialist revolutions. Kaufmann examines the influences of Christian ideas and European society on socialism to give a fuller picture of the movement at the turn of the century as well as offers his predictions for the future of socialism in Europe. This title is ideal for students of sociology and history, particularly students interested in the development of modern intellectual and social movements.

Socialism and Modern Thought

M. Kaufmann

First published in 1895
by Methuen & Co. Ltd

This edition first published in 2016 by Routledge
2 Park Square, Milton Park, Abingdon, Oxon, OX14 4RN
and by Routledge
711 Third Avenue, New York, NY 10017

Routledge is an imprint of the Taylor & Francis Group, an informa business

© 1895, Methuen & Co. Ltd

All rights reserved. No part of this book may be reprinted or reproduced or utilised in any form or by any electronic, mechanical, or other means, now known or hereafter invented, including photocopying and recording, or in any information storage or retrieval system, without permission in writing from the publishers.

Publisher's Note
The publisher has gone to great lengths to ensure the quality of this reprint but points out that some imperfections in the original copies may be apparent.

Disclaimer
The publisher has made every effort to trace copyright holders and welcomes correspondence from those they have been unable to contact.

A Library of Congress record exists under LC control number: 11021208

ISBN 13: 978-1-138-18716-0 (hbk)
ISBN 13: 978-1-315-64330-4 (ebk)
ISBN 13: 978-1-138-18719-1 (pbk)

SOCIALISM AND MODERN THOUGHT

BY

M. KAUFMANN, M.A.

Rector of Ingworth and Vicar of Calthorpe, Norfolk

AUTHOR OF "SOCIALISM, ITS NATURE, ITS DANGER, AND ITS REMEDIES," ETC., ETC.

METHUEN & CO.
36, ESSEX STREET, W.C.
LONDON
1895

CONTENTS

CHAPTER		PAGE
	PREFACE	VI
	INTRODUCTION	VII
I.	THE PHYLOSOPHY OF SOCIALISM	1
II.	SOCIALISM AND DARWINISM	17
III.	MORALITIES OF SOCIALISM	38
IV.	PESSIMISM AND SOCIALISTIC OPTIMISM	60
V.	SOCIALISM AND POSITIVISM	79
VI.	SOCIALISM AND CULTURE	102
VII.	ART AND ANARCHY	119
VIII.	SOCIALISM AND ROMANISM	130
IX.	SOCIALISM AND PROTESTANTISM	153
	SUMMARY AND CONCLUSION	174

PREFACE

Some of the contents of chapters I—IV have already appeared in the *Church Quarterly* and *London Quarterly Reviews* and chapter VII in the *National Review*. Everything, however, has been re-cast and to a great extent re-written, and is in no sense a mere reproduction of magazine articles. The remainder of the book contains entirely new matter, a footnote here and there indicating passages where a slight use has been made of former contributions to periodical literature by the author.

INTRODUCTION

> "Der Socialismus ist die mit klarem Bewusstsein und voller Erkenntniss auf alle Gebiete menschlicher Thätigkeit angewandte Wissenschaft."
>
> A. BEBEL.

NUMEROUS works have appeared within the last ten years on modern socialism, but the writer of this is not aware that anyone has shown the connection between the movement and the general current of thought, extending over the whole field of intellectual activity in the present day. And yet the true meaning of the socialistic movement cannot be understood without some comprehensive view of the age we live in, its philosophy of life, its leading scientific theories, its ethical conceptions, its peculiar mood of agnostic pessimism, its determined effort to perform the practical duties of life in spite of the weariness of spirit which comes of lost faith, its willingness to take up a standpoint on the sure ground of positive fact only, and its consequent preference for the Religion of Humanity or the Religion of Culture as substitutes for traditional creeds.

Without presuming to treat exhaustively the various aspects of these vast conglomerate themes, each of which could well fill a volume by itself, the present writer endeavours here to supply in a measure, at least, this deficiency in socialistic literature. And since a survey of the history of socialism shows that at all critical epochs of human thought and life it appears and re-appears as the outcome of the *Zeitgeist* more or less connected with contemporary religious movements, so now it cannot be dissociated from modern religious thought and Christian ideas in modern shape, as moral and intellectual forces among others influencing the current of the social movement. In this way we may regard as nearly as possible the principal factors of Modern Thought in their relation to the social problem, and this may help us in measuring more accurately the relative force and direction of these tendencies in their mutual action and reaction. Having ascertained more clearly what the various influences are which are imperceptibly shaping at this moment the present and future destiny of European society, we may the better individually and collectively contribute our own share in the thought and work of the hour. It is a well-known fact to students of great revolutionary movements that a better knowledge of the intellectual and spiritual forces in operation in their life-time would have enabled the actors and spectators of the revolutionary era to modify, if not to avert these outbreaks of popular passion in the past.

In the same way a more accurate conception of the prevalent moods of thought and feeling in our own day, and of those religious ideas which pervade our mental atmosphere and from which unconsciously social ideas take their colouring and are sustained in their aspiration, may assist us in turning the stream of socialistic thought into safer channels and by means of timely reforms to avert a social revolution. A careful study of all current movements, together with that of socialism which professes to be no less than a complete theory of life and mind, * will help in pointing out to us our duty to think, feel, speak, and act in such a manner as to secure, as far as possible, the real welfare of society now and in the immediate future.

* "Der Socialismus ist Religion und Wissenschaft zugleich — als Sache des Gefühls und Gewissens hat er die ganze Stärke des Christenthums, als Sache des Verstandes hat er die Stärke der Wissenschaft."— W. LIEBKNECHT.

SOCIALISM AND MODERN THOUGHT

CHAPTER I

THE PHILOSOPHY OF SOCIALISM

> Socialism is the Philosophy of Political Economy of the working classes.
> VON SCHEEL.

Is there such a thing as the Philosophy of Socialism? If by philosophy we understand the tendency to look for the causes of things, and to look forward to their consequences, and thence to deduce principles of conduct in the present which shall be conducive to the social welfare of the Humanity of the future, there can be no doubt that some socialists, the men of light and leading among them, are social philosophers of a kind. Militant socialism has its non-combatants, its men of thought as well as its men of deed. Unlike the philosophers who followed Napoleon's army in the Egyptian campaign and ordered as soon as the square was formed for action "*Philosophes au milieu!*" the philosophers of socialism are always in the front, as its scientific explorers; they are more—they are its spiritual commanders. The whole campaign is conducted according to their theories. Besides this their followers, too, have their moments of reflection as well as their seasons of restless agitation; they follow more or less the reflective tendency of the age, and we are all of us philosophers in the present day. We all observe, not always correctly, perhaps, we collect facts and on them we generalize, sometimes rather hastily, and so we frame theories of life and the universe, of ethics and politics, of social life and religion according to our prepossessions, and the socialist only does what the rest of the world do. Now philosophy, a generalized view of men, things, and principles, differs according to the standpoint we occupy. In this way the socialist has his own peculiar philosophy of the universe and human history, and on this he builds up his theory of society. He has his own moral philosophy with its bearings on altruistic duty. He has his philosophy of political justice affecting the modifiability of the laws of property, and he has his own ideals too, and his own philosophic views on the religion of the future. In short he is not a stranger altogether to the "philosophic mind," though his way of philosophizing is different from that of the Doctors of Philosophy and their disciples who are not socialists, and this difference is important to the last degree.

For, as has been pointed out by a well-known German writer on the subject, it amounts to a revolution of ideas, and intellectual revolutions, as the French Revolution has taught us, are apt to precede important political and social changes. For this reason a short sketch of socialist philosophy, cosmical, historical, ethical, political and religious, is given at the forefront of this volume as the best introduction to a more detailed account of the connection between socialism and modern thought.

1. Now, in the first place this philosophy is of a pronounced materialistic type. We do not say that all socialists entertain a mechanical view of the universe,

some do not trouble themselves about the universe at all, and many in the rank and file of socialism are spiritualist in philosophy, but the foremost thinkers among them endorse the saying of Karl Marx that "the ideal for me is simply the material as transmuted in the human mind," or they accept the saying of a recent writer in the high-toned *Revue Socialiste* in an article entitled "*L'âme de Demain*": "I believe in science and I believe in the ideal. Science makes me what I am, and I make my ideal what it is." * That is, the ideal is found in the actual and nowhere else. "Sensible actual reality is our ideal; the ideal of Social-Democracy is materialistic" is the frank confession of another disciple of K. Marx. The modern socialist is quite free from those

> "Blank misgivings of a creature
> Moving about in worlds unrealized"

of which the poet speaks, simply because those

> "High instincts, before which our mortal Nature
> Doth tremble like a guilty thing surprised,"

are to him naught else but the "immaterial fancies of a disordered brain." In fact nature has no terror for him except the possibility of an empty stomach, or a temporary stoppage in the supply of the "actual bodily wants of an existence worthy of a human being", which, he tells us, is "the last ground" on which "the justice, truth and reason of Social-Democracy rest". Anarchists, as far as they are philosophers, simply adopt the atomistic theory of the scientists and in it see the *raison d'être* of individual autonomy.—What they ask for is complete freedom of action for each social atom, similar to the free play of mechani-

* Revue Socialiste, Tome 14. No. 82, p. 391.

cal forces and molecules moving about freely in the physical universe. Collectivists as believers in organized development rely on the power of human will to modify the social structure and on the rights of collective humanity to conquer natural obstacles to human progress. But they, too, regard the whole of social life as a purely natural process, "a simultaneous movement of absorption and excretion" of protoplasm.

2. Such is the "Economic Materialism" of modern socialism. Its philosophy of history is a direct outcome of this. "History is simply the sum total of changes in the powers of production, that is, a history of the struggle for existence between social classes." Socialists taking advantage of the historical method try to show that human history is a purely mechanical process brought about by physical causes, depending at every successive stage on the existing modes of production and distribution of the necessaries of life, that the exertion of will is conditioned by material processes in the nervous centres, that the history of the world is a "physico-chemical process" and so forth. At the same time it is felt that to explain historical progress by natural selection, heredity, and adaptation and to adopt the theories of materialistic evolutionists pure and simple may prove rather inconvenient to the establishment of the socialist doctrine. For if they are true they lead to consequences which do not suit the socialist argument. And it is curious to note the shifts to which socialists are reduced in seeking to escape from them. So long as their doctrines militate against established beliefs and the social institutions founded on them they are welcomed as helpful in bringing about an intellectual revolution, with important practical results.

But, as Darwinists and others have not been slow to recognize, the more shrewd among the socialists do not fail to see that the doctrine of natural selection is not in favour of Democracy; that, on the contrary, its tendency is aristocratic; and that, like the theological doctrine of Election, it speaks of "an elect fragment of the human race", a favoured minority, a remnant saved in the survival of the fittest. They even go so far as to complain of the "fatalities of Nature", which bring about a "social predestination" that accounts for the existence of privileged persons and classes. The natural history of man may be a triumph of mind over matter, but the process of social evolution, culminating in social equality, is often retarded. How then can all this be explained on socialist principles? According to the socialist philosophy of history the differentiation of classes began at the point where human productivity created more commodities than were required for immediate use. This made possible a laying up in stock for the future what practically amounted to the accumulation of capital. Diversities of fortunes produced differences of position and distinction of class. These increased with the increase of wealth. As civilization became more complex it led to further specialization of social functions and division of labour for economic and political reasons. Thus was brought about a separation of classes and social disintegration, where class-hatred and class conflicts prevail; in short, history in its final development brings the social problem to a point. It is left for us to solve the problem, and for the historian of the future to say how it was done. At present the sub-division of labour and the introduction of machinery increase every hour the power of capital, and enable the employer to rob the employed of their due, to take the lion's share in the shape of profit, and to leave a pittance to the worker according to the price of labour in the market. Thus man, following his natural instincts, errs from the path of right, but the time is coming when the rights of men will be recognized and the wrongs of society redressed. If, as the old economists said, man is a machine, the modern opponents of capitalism say he is also a self-regulating machine. When he makes mistakes, and the social machinery gets out of gear, he can put things in order again in his own way. Then the time comes in the course of historical evolution when social usurpation will no longer be tolerated, when those who have the biggest clubs and form the largest body in a society where club-law reigns will know how to use their power in putting an end to the rule of the industrial oppressor. Among the forces of Nature there is, also, the force of resistance and, corresponding to cataclysms and catastrophes in Nature, there is the crash of revolutions in social systems.

Such was the course of reasoning employed by one of the principal speakers at the *Congrès National des Syndicats Ouvriers* at Lyons in 1887 and he concluded his address in the following words:—

"Let us remember that we are so numerous that nothing can resist us, especially when we have force for our means and justice for our end."

In a calmer and more philosophic tone Agathon de Potter in his brochure *La Révolution prédite* republished from *La Philosophie de l'avenir* in the same year, remarks:—

"Those who object to the present organization are
"already more numerous and will soon be more powerful

"than they who profit by it. Yes, the *bourgeois* society
"is irremediably lost; in a not distant future it will pass
"away. But the social transformation may be effected
"either peacefully, or violently, either in a way that shall
"injure no one, or in a way that will produce incalculable
"harm. Only, in order that the change may be effected
"peacefully and safely, the ruling classes must put themselves
"at the head of the movement. At present it would seem
"that their intellectual shortsightedness renders them
"incapable of taking part in this pacific social reformation.
"Should this feeble-mindedness continue, it can only be
"by anarchy and by the evils that anarchy will bring to
"their persons and their property that they can be
"constrained to seek, to find, and to supply those measures
"that are needed for the destruction of pauperism."

This is the "crash of doom" which is predicted on the principles of historical necessity—social dissolution as far as the present society is concerned, as the next stage in social evolution and the next chapter of "universal history from a socialist standpoint." But what next? Here the philosophy of socialism ends in a *cul-de-sac*, no further changes are required after capitalism has ended in collectivism, in the succeeding æons of socialistic rule.

Here we note the influence of Hegel's philosophy, even in its imperfections. Karl Marx, himself, notes with his usual accuracy this fault in the reasonings of his master and points to the contradiction between Hegel's view of the dialectical process of history leading to ever-increasing perfection, and his evident assumption that this process was to culminate in his own philosophical system, as the absolute truth. Yet Marx and his socialist disciples repeat the same mistake in taking for granted that the dialectical process of history ends in the socialist state, when according to Engels, his lifelong friend and executor, the proletarian revolution shall have finally solved the last of the series of historical contradictions, and men at length will be masters of their own form of social organization, having become lords of creation and masters of themselves. In this, he thinks, consists the historical vocation of the modern proletariat, to bring about the great world deliverance, which is "the transformation of the civilized or state world into a socialized or communal world". *

3. "Morals without Metaphysics" is the watchword of the day, and attempts of a high order are being made to find a scientific basis of ethics. The moral philosophy of scientific socialism embraces this modern view of ethics, but at the same time exaggerates the importance of its realistic groundwork, and excludes too rigidly the ideal factors from this "new morality". Its own morality is "rooted in the earth", resting on a purely physical foundation. ethical conceptions, according to this view, are merely the reflection of actual conditions in the economic environment. The spiritual nature of man is either denied, or explained as a mental mirage of outward things, whilst moral evolution is only a process of cerebral modifications. Thus the ideas of justice, liberty, and utility, so far from being accounted the antecedent causes, are rather the concomitants or consequences of external conditions. Circumstances make us what we are; the status determines the habit of the social organism. In this ethical conception of the origin and development of ethics socialists prefer to follow Mr. Darwin's teaching, that the "moral sense

* Die Entwickelung des Socialismus von der Utopia zur Wissenschaft, von Friedrich Engels, p. 49.

is fundamentally identical with the social instincts". In this sense, at least, the words are quoted in a little volume entitled "*A Working Man's Philosophy*" by *One of the Crowd*. That such was the opinion held by the precursors of the French Revolution is well known, and Sir Henry S. Maine, in his work on "*Ancient Law*" has pointed out the serious error of Montesquieu as one of them in having "looked on the nature of man as entirely plastic, as passively reproducing the impressions, and submitting implicitly to the impulses which he received from without," and in thus greatly underrating "the stability of human nature".*

Similarly in the view of modern socialists, a series of social formations, changing according to circumstances, is accompanied by a series of moral transformations, and by a similar transmutation of ideas affecting the law of property, ethical conceptions undergo change with important bearings on the social organism, its growth and development. Thus individualism, which has produced the present state of things described "as one of tumultuous progress", is being undermined by various efforts to displace it by the creation of associative forms of industry, but this is in consequence of a revolution, an evolution in contemporary ethics, altruism asserting itself as against egoism, the doctrine of self-interest pure and simple being discredited and that of the common interests of the whole community entering more fully into the conscience of civilized nations. So much so, indeed, that according to this new philosophy moral duty, as a whole, resolves itself into an endeavour to promote the social well-being by means of a collective

* *Ancient Law*, 6th E., p. 116; The opposite error of Rousseau is pointed out on pp. 88—89 of the same work, and its serious consequences in the course of the Revolution, pp. 91—276.

solidarity. Here the only motive force of moral conduct is love of the species, and the highest moral sanction is the law of the social commonwealth: "Solidarity between human beings, and universal sympathy, or, at least, the constant endeavour to save every living being from useless suffering; is not this human morality *par excellence?* Socialists cannot chose a better." So far the modern socialist simply adopts the current views of ethical teachers whose system rests on a real basis of science. But such a view does not square with the "class morality" held up as the socialist ideal which is preached in most of the organs of social democracy of the present day. "We believe," said the editor of *L'Egalité* on its first appearance as the organ of modern collectivism, "with the collectivist school, to which all serious minds of the proletariat in both hemispheres belong to-day, that the natural and scientific evolution of humanity is bearing it irresistibly to the collective appropriation of the soil and the instruments of labour." Such a statement which makes the material good of man the *summum bonum* of existence presents us with a low moral ideal inconsistent with the boasted superiority of the "Ethics of reason."

We are told, with a moral bluntness which strangely contrasts with a profession of lofty social aims, that "to the socialist labour is an evil to be minimized to the utmost, the man who works at his trade or avocation more than necessity compels him, or who accumulates more than he can enjoy, is not a hero, but a fool, from the socialist standpoint, and thrift is contemptuously discarded." It does not require much penetration to see that a society where labour and thrift are condemned, or treated with supreme contumely, would scarcely be the best kind of environment to prepare the mind for the sacrifice of personal interest to social duty, the kind of altruism on which the socialist philosopher would found his socialist state.

4. When we turn from the ethical to the political philosophy of socialism, we find the same practical application of the new laws of morality to consist in the confiscation of all the powers of production in order to prevent the future exploitation of the producing classes by "profit mongers". Expropriation becomes "political justice", for it only amounts to a restoration of stolen property to the original owners since all the instruments of labour and capital (itself nothing else but congealed labour) are the products of former work. All is to be held in trust by the state and "what we mean by the state is the objectivation of realization of justice, having for its highest aim the material and moral welfare of the citizen". There is no such thing as the rights of property, *i.e.* private property, except that founded in its previous acquisition by labour.

Nature does not acknowledge any ownership save that which is the result of individual exertion, in her sight all occupy the same rights, the sacredness of labour alone constitutes the sacredness of property.* It is forgotten here that "just laws do not exclude unequal fortunes", though it may be the duty of just governments to restrain the forces of unprincipled cupidity which prevents any of its citizens from fully developing their powers in the attempt to adapt themselves to their environment. For the true justification of property lies in the principle that

* Henry George: *Progress and Poverty*, pp. 300—301 (2nd Ed.). Cf. Karl Frohme: Die Entwickelung der Eigenthumsverhältnisse, pp. 170—173; 178.

it forms the material environment for due self-development of the *propria persona*, and this self-development is necessary for the due performance of the social functions of every individual. Advanced reformers and others expect much from the growing tendency gradually to displace individual by co-operative enterprise, and from the substitution of collective from private property, resulting therefrom, and this process would no doubt lead to a modification of our property laws. They, therefore, demand legislative protection, if not governmental aid, as a measure of public security, and much may be done by the legislature in the way of protecting and encouraging, without directly promoting, co-operation. As Von Scheel, in an article on the latest acts of legislation in Germany, tersely puts it: "Modern social legislation must make it its object to bring about an equation between political and social development.... to introduce, as far as this can be done, equality, not theoretical but real, and without, in doing so, breaking with the recognised principles of social order as far as this is possible." *

5. In the last place we must state briefly what is the attitude of socialists generally towards Christianity and show what is their philosophy of religion.

Religion is declared in some of their programmes to be a matter of indifference, though practically the socialist tendency is to regard Christianity as an effete system of religious thought, suitable to past ages of ignorance, but inconsistent with prevalent modes of thought and utterly incapable of supplying the spiritual needs of the society of the future. "The working classes," says Mr. Belfort Bax in his book on "*The Religion of Socialism*," "see

* Unsere Zeit, 1887, Heft. 1, p. 114.

plainly enough that Christianity in all its forms belongs to the world of the past and the present, but not to that world of the future which is to bring universal emancipation." As in the socialized world of the future social utility takes the place of personal beliefs, so, too, "Atheistic Humanism" will replace Christian grace. In this way Socialism represents the "typical Aryan ethics" as distinguished from the "typical Semitic ethics."

Here, too, socialism in its modern form, as the child of Hegelianism in Philosophy, is essentially critical and evolutionary. Religion is the result, too, of historical development. The era of Paganism, the religion of slave industry; that of Catholicism, the religion of suffrage; and then Protestantism, the religion of capitalism, succeed each other in the joint result of social and moral evolution. In due course of time comes Humanism with its "religion of collective and co-operative industry" (p. 81).

As in the coming international republic, the social instincts will be rehabilitated by a return to the manners and customs of primitive society transcendentalized by modern science, so the religious instincts are to be transformed by a return to the Atheism of the children of Nature, before creeds and dogmas were invented by priestly impostors and political usurpers. "Religion," according to Dietzgen, the German philosopher-tanner, "is primitive world-wisdom. Social-Democracy, on the contrary, is the product of the process still going on of an ever-growing development of culture having its root in remote antiquity." The Most High of this latest product of religious philosophy is, we are told in his lay sermons on the religion of social-democracy, civilized Humanity. Our own mind or spirit is the only supreme being. "Conscious labour, or planned organization of social labour, is the name of the expected Messiah of the new age. Our hope of salvation is not a religious ideal, but rests on the massive foundation-stone of Materialism."

From this it will appear that socialists are not likely to be led away by the error of *bourgeois* religion, which according to one of their number is *reverence*. We no longer believe in a Creator, but only ourselves as the makers of our future and the founders of our destiny and we most devoutly worship this new Creator. In the "anthropocentric" universe of this philosophy there is "no other religion but the social-democratic theory, founded on a purely materialistic view of the Universe." "When man has learned to be his own organizer," concludes the writer referred to, "the place of religion is supplied by the religion of social-democracy." If it be said that "man must have a religion"—that must be changed into "Man must have a system". Such is the new gospel of socialism. "The city of pigs" was Plato's first but by no means last ideal of the Republic. It would seem from what we have said that it is the last word of Socialism steeped in the morass of Materialism from which modern thought is being gradually released and rescued by a return to spirituality. It is only fair, however, to state that such is by no means the universally accepted theory of religion among the rank and file of the socialist body. There are many among them who look upon the course of nature and history as more than a meaningless muddle of mechanical movements. To K. Marx the ideal was nothing but "material facts turned up and down in the human head", but the materialistic view of man and the Universe is not essential to modern socialism as an economic system. *

And as has been said when "the work of Karl Marx has been forgotten as a curiosity of economic speculation and as a masterly exposition of some of the evils of the present competition system, socialism as an ideal of political and social reform may continue to awake as much enthusiasm as before." †

But without religion, as Saint Simon declared on his deathbed, there can be no enthusiasm for ideals, and the founder of Christianity has been called by a socialist the "Undying Idealist". Mr. Kidd in his recent work on Social Evolution has again emphasized the fact that religion is "the central feature of human history", and that its phenomena "constitute one of the most persistent and characteristic features of human society" (p: 87), and that the "suprarational" sanction it provides for conduct is essentially necessary as a form in social development. And the foundation and spread of a Labour Church in the North, and its object as described by its founder, are an illustration of the truth that the spiritual side of human nature cannot be satisfied without religious ideals and the inspiration of religious thought and feeling.

"The Labour Church is an organized effort," so runs the preface of its hymn-book, "to develop the religious "life inherent in the labour movement, and to give to "that movement a higher inspiration and a sturdier "independence in the great work of personal and social "regeneration that lies before it. It appeals especially to "those who have abandoned the traditional religion of the

* Bonar, James—Philosophy and Political Economy, p. 393, cf. p. 528—329.

† Mackenzie, J. S.—An Introduction to Social Philosophy, p. 275.

"day without having found satisfaction in abandoning religion
"altogether. The Message of the Labour Church is that
"without obedience to God's laws there can be no liberty.
"The Gospel of the Labour Church is that God is in the
"labour movement, working through it for the farther emanci-
"pation of man from the tyranny, both of his own half-
"developed nature, and of those social conditions, which are
"opposed to his higher development. The Call of the Labour
"Church is to men everywhere to become God's fellow-workers
"in the Era of Reconstruction on which we have entered." *

But what religion? it may be asked. Perhaps, as Dr. Mackenzie puts it, we want a new Christ. That is scarcely necessary. Thus far the Christian religion, adapting itself to varying conditions of successive social development, has been found sufficient for the purpose of elevating and energizing man in his various efforts towards social improvement. It is not the religious system which is at fault, but the spirit in which it is understood and applied by some of its professors. What we want is not a new religion or a new philosophy of it, but a renewal of the real Christianity as propounded in the Sermon on the Mount and in the Epistle to the Philippians by St. Paul. What we now want is simply "an accession of the Christ-like spirit, the spirit of self-devotion to ideal ends." †

* Quoted in letter from John Trevor to *Spectator*, April 28, 1894. See ib. April 21st, A graphic account of the Labour Church by Miss Evelyn March-Philipps. Also the Labour Annual for 1895, pp. 42 seq.

† Mackenzie loc. cit. p. 377.

So, too, Lieutenant-Colonel M. von Egidy in his remarkable brochure on *Earnest Reflections*, published in 1891 and producing quite a sensation in Germany, says: "Christian thought is not to be altered, all that is required is to bring back Christianity to its original truth; this is not innovation, not even 'alteration', or amendment, it is '*restoration*'."

CHAPTER II

SOCIALISM AND DARWINISM

> "Le Darwinisme appliqué aux sciences morales rejette toute idée d'egalité et glorifie le triomphe du plus fort ou du plus habile."
> E. CARO.

MODERN thought is saturated with what is popularly understood under the term of Darwinism, and, as we have already noticed in the preceding chapter, there is a decided tendency among socialist writers to base their own theory on scientific data. So, here, we have to point out how in framing a system of society, as it is to be, the assumed or ascertained laws of social biology and evolution are called into requisition, and social revolution itself is represented as part of the process of transformation and modification which the social organism has to pass through in order to complete its social development. In so far as this view regards the life and growth of social organisms as part of the general process of life in the material universe, it is identical with modern thought which tends to regard all phenomena as subject to the mechanical laws of Nature. What distinguishes the socialist view of natural laws and sequences in social evolution is the peculiar interpretation of those laws and their practical application. Here we find that science is sometimes called in as a witness to support the claims of "Scientific Socialism", at other times as an ally in its revolt against the existing order of things, and as furnishing a new basis of social reconstruction. It is in reference to this that one of the advanced writers on the subject says that since the days of Copernicus there has been no doctrine proclaimed of a more revolutionary character than that of Darwin, whilst another says that the revolution in economics brought about by Marx is the same as that effected in science by Darwin. It is well, therefore, to inquire how far the distinctive doctrines of Darwinism and Socialism touch and intersect each other, and, also, what may be the effect of the contrary or concurrent tendencies of the two movements, both of them forming a very powerful element in the course of modern thought in its effect on social life.*

Natural revivals in Philosophy are generally accompanied by realistic views of life. Epicureanism flourished in the times of Gassendi and Holbach, and mainly because the progress of natural science is generally accompanied or preceded by a considerable increase of the means of indulgence. But an increased desire after material indulgence among the lower strata of society is one of the

* It has been noticed that the year 1859 which saw the publication of the Origin of Species was also the year in which Marx published the "*Critique of Political Economy*" which contains in *nuce* the ideas of the "*Kapital*" published in 1869.

In the former work Marx says distinctly: 1, that the structure of society is the real basis on which the legal and political superstructure is raised, and 2, that the modes of producing the material necessaries of life determine the process of social, political, and spiritual life development.

elements, at least, of socialism. So, too, in our own days we have to take account of a form of "vulgar Darwinism", which undoubtedly lends encouragement to low social ideals among all classes. To give an example or two: Take the following quotation from one of the organs of the *parti ouvrier*, *i.e.* the party of moderate socialism in France: "Materialism," says the writer, ".... is the basis of scientific and international socialism. It is because Karl Marx was a materialist that he looks on the whole course of history as a struggle of classes, as according to Darwin life itself is a struggle for existence; this is materialism." * So also this from the pen of Prince Krapotkine, the advocate of social anarchy: "It is not enough to have a noble ideal: man cannot live on great thoughts and lofty discourses alone; he requires bread; the stomach has more rights than even the brain, for it is the stomach which sustains the whole organism." † But this is only one view of the subject. According to another, Darwinism helps to give point to the higher aspirations of socialism and to raise new hopes of their speedy fulfilment. Thus Emile Gautier in his brochure, entitled *Le Darwinisme Social*, states the case clearly and succinctly. "All social, political and moral phenomena are, like the rest, subject to natural laws." But so far from Darwin's law authorizing the reign of competition and thus giving its sanction to *exploiteurs* he considers that it contains a new and most powerful argument in favour of socialism.

He maintains 1. that the conditions of Darwin's law are modifiable like other laws of nature, and will be transformed with the prodigious development of human intelligence and activity in modern civilization.

* *Le Socialiste*, Deuxième année, No. 42.
† *Expropriation*, an anarchic essay by Peter Krapotkine, p. 1.

2. That, instead of submitting passively to the "fatalities of nature", human will reacts against them and will finally gain the dominion over nature.

3. That the fatalities which crush us are conventional, "*fatalités artificielles*", "*fatalités sociales*".

4. That it is not nature, but society which distributes social advantages and disadvantages, and that society, which after all is a human creation, is subject to human revision.

5. That society is not what it should be, because it fails to correct the fatalities of nature from which human beings suffer.

6. That revolutionary socialism demands the reformation of society on the ground that change and modifiability are the principal conditions of Darwin's theory.

Such is the "skeleton of the argument". Like other skeletons it reminds society of its moribund condition. Reduced to the most simple terms it really amounts to this, that the morphological laws of nature as taught in Darwinism are opposed to the immutability of human institutions; that variation of types in the physical world corresponds to modifications in the structure and functions of social organisms, and that it is the mission of socialism to bring them about.

At first sight, indeed, M. Gautier admits that Darwinism appears to favour privilege and inequality. But the theory, when thoroughly understood and pushed to its extreme consequences, lends a most important though unexpected support to revolutionary socialism. True, man is an animal, and, as such, subject to the ordinary laws of adaptation and environment in the struggle for existence, the laws of natural selection and heredity which seriously affect the feeble and less skilful. But then, he is "*un animal spécial, intelligent, sociable, relativement libre*", whose faculties have reached such a degree of superior intensity as to bring about, in his case, results altogether different from those effected among the lower animals by the operation of the same laws. He is in possession of a personal force which tends to manifest itself spontaneously, and to counterbalance those blind forces which formerly dominated, and do so still in some measure, the less favoured species. This, M. Gautier insists, is the key of the whole argument. Man masters nature not by abrogating her laws, but by means of introducing new conditions. His own "mechanism" assists as an additional factor. As in the case of the laws of electricity, here also he shapes to his own will the course of nature in observing her laws, and he can change that course by his scientific skill in every other case. The formation of society itself is such a reaction against the crude laws of nature; for society exists for the very purpose of protecting the feeble, whom blind natural force would crush, against the strong, that is those whom they favour. The altruistic spirit of human solidarity is in direct antagonism to the egotistical instinct of natural self-preservation. In the savage state, or state of nature, indeed, the struggle for existence, or the law of the strongest, reigns supreme, and subsequently artificial arrangements are introduced by the strong in possession so as to perpetuate such inequalities in favour of their progeny, who may be utterly destitute of the physical or intellectual superiority to which their progenitors owe their origin. Thus obstacles are introduced to *prevent the free play of competition*, because all do not start with the same advantages; the naturally gifted have no chance against those who, without natural endowments, are placed in superior social position by birth and early training. This constitutes not "natural selection", but "artificial selection", social not natural fatalities determine the fortune of the rich fool and poor man of genius—not natural causes but "*causes voulus*"; not natural conditions, but factitious circumstances, in which labour, diligence, and capacity play but a secondary part, are responsible for the result. Society, in short, not nature, is guilty of the wrong done to its less favoured members, since its legal, political, and economical arrangements are quite arbitrary. Were the true measure of a man's value, "*le dynamètre de la valeur individuelle*", *i.e.* labour and the power of production, strictly applied, no room would be left for useless members of society—that is, for those who are our present masters.

This amounts to an acquittal of nature and an accusation of society. Accordingly society is warned to mend its ways. It is told not to put its faith in a "social predestination", which condemns some of its members to perpetual suffering for no fault of theirs, but to remove all conventional impediments to the free development of the natural gifts of all. For if not, repressed energies will assert their natural rights by an appeal to brutal force, one of the forces of impartial nature for the protection of the disinherited. The alternatives are either self-rectification or self-destruction, social reform, or the suicide of society. The final victory of man over nature will be brought about by the complete consecration of all human efforts to the good of all. And, "*il faut organiser la lutte contre la lutte pour vivre.*" That is, concerted action in the place of individual conflict, the harmonizing of natural inequalities with distributive justice, and an equivalence of force brought about by generous and sympathetic action—in short a common alliance against natural oppression under the standard of a confederated universe—such a new fellowship of social life, in which all difficulties could be effaced and compensation made for all inequalities, would once more restore to society, as a whole, the common heritage of past generations of men, who each have had their own share in its creation and transmission to us, the heirs of all the ages.

This is the position taken up by Socialism in its relation to Darwinism. It will be interesting, in the next place, to see how far these friendly advances are met by Darwinists in defining their own attitudes towards Socialism. Two distinguished exponents of Darwinism in Germany, whose translated works are well known in this country, have spoken authoritatively on the subject. Both declare in the most unequivocal manner, that Darwinism gives no support whatever to the leading principles of "Scientific Socialism". Oscar Schmidt, late Professor of Zoology at the University of Strassburg, the well-known author of the "Doctrine of Descent and Darwinism" which forms the twelfth volume of the International Scientific Series, said, in a published address delivered before the 51st Meeting of Scientists and Physicians at Cassel in 1878—the year in which socialism reached its zenith in Germany—

"The result of our enquiry is this, that the Social-
"Democracy when it appeals to Darwinism, does not fathom
"its meaning, and when, in exceptional cases, it does, it
"seems to be at a loss what to do with it, compelled as
"it finds itself to deny its essential principle, competi-
"tion" (p. 38).

An address delivered before the same body in the previous year by Professor E. Haeckel had provoked the adverse criticism of Professor Virchow and, in the course of a notorious controversy which followed thereupon, Haeckel published a reply under the heading "Freedom in Science and Teaching," which subsequently appeared in an English dress, and in which Haeckel strives to show the utter "incompatibility between the doctrines of Socialism and Darwinism." "It is exactly," he says, "the theory of descent which more than any other theory of science predicates in the most unqualified terms the impossibility of equality." O. Schmidt, in the pamphlet already referred to, clenches the whole matter positively and negatively by denying any doctrinal affinity between Socialism and Darwinism in the following aphoristic declaration:

1. Darwinism is the scientific proof of inequality.

2. Any reference to such axioms as that man is originally good, and that natural science compels us to regard each individual as *equally capable of the same development*, finds no support anywhere in Darwinistic literature.

After this it is unnecessary to enter into further details of the controversy between Socialism and Darwinism, or to discuss special points of it, except, perhaps, the question how far individualism or socialism receives any support from the analogy of "the social instincts", which lead to certain forms of association amongst the lower animals. Here, again, there is conflict not conformity of opinion between the scientists and the socialists, the latter stoutly affirming, the former vigorously denying, that we meet collective forms of life or associated labour among the higher classes of the animal world. It is from communistic to individual forms of life that the animal creation advances, say the scientists. It is only among superior animals, such as the elephant and the beaver, that we notice the first beginnings of solidarity, say the socialists; the tape worm, "*ver solitaire,*" is the prototype of individualism lower down the scale of animal life. We need not enter into these controversies. Enough has been said to make it plain that the representatives of Darwinism are as anxious to deny the logical connection of their theories with those of socialism as the exponents of the latter are anxious to affirm it. As might be expected from the nature of the case, the recipients of rejected addresses have grown less amiable in consequence and a tone of acrimonious acerbity has crept into later discussions on the subject. Thus Lafargue in his "*Course d'Économie Sociale*", which forms part of the *Bibliothèque Socialiste*, speaks contemptuously of the servility of scientific men, whilst he accuses the followers of Darwin of actually falsifying the teachings of science and degrading them into instruments of oppression. In the approved French *façon de parler*: "Be my brother, or I will kill thee," Lafargue dwells with approbation on the murder of the great scientist Lavoisier, holding him up as a warning to scientific men of the present day who wilfully reject the fraternal advances of socialism, or even go so far as to question the soundness of its teachings. In the same way Gabriel Deville, in the introduction to his epitome of K. Marx's book on Capital, accentuates with evident relish, though in guarded terms, the consequences of admitting Darwin's theory of the rule of the stronger in the struggle for existence as the *dura lex sed lex* in the economic world, by forcibly reminding society and its scientific preceptors that the masses of the people have the strongest arms, and can use them should there be occasion for hard blows. In one of the *Petites Publications Anarchistes*, entitled "*La Révolution et l'Autonomie selon la Science*" the same idea is expressed in all its brutal simplicity: "*Nous sommes les plus forts.... vous l'avez dit vous-même: la victoire est aux plus forts!*"

However, it must not be supposed that this appeal to force, as a corrollary from the doctrine of the struggle for existence ending in the survival of the strongest, is the only argument of militant socialism. On the contrary, a great deal of logical ingenuity is displayed in the special pleadings of socialism founded on Darwinism, in which the latter is dragged in as a witness against its will in the contention of socialism with society. Thus, when Haeckel and Schmidt deduce the doctrine of inequality from their own scientific date, socialists admit, indeed, that inequality results from the struggle for existence. But why? Because competition among human beings is totally different from the struggle for existence among plants and animals. In the former it is the struggle of employers among themselves as to who shall beat the other in the markets of the world, but it is the labourer's back which suffers from the conflict. His wages are lowered, his hours of labour prolonged, his wife and children used up in the factory to cheapen production and to heighten profits. In the animal and vegetable world competition among equals evolves higher degrees of adaptation and efficiency: not so in the world of human beings. Here, on the contrary, it ends in the physical degeneration and the moral and mental degradation of the wage-earning classes. The cases are not analogous from any point of view. The arms used in the struggle and the battle-ground selected for it are entirely dissimilar; hence, too, the results must be so. Animals fight with the arms provided by nature, which form part of their organism. In the case of man they are an artificial appendage. Those who use them have not acquired them by their own effort and skill, except in a few cases, and thus in the course of time the struggle assumes the character of a war of classes that becomes more intensified in the course of human development. What socialism demands is not a uniformity of conditions; it admits natural, muscular, and cerebral inequalities, and is too scientific to deny heterogeneity as a condition of progress. What socialism demands is equality in the use of means of development, an equal access to the instruments of activity, equality to start with. Adaptation to environment leads, no doubt, to higher development among animals and plants. But in the case of human beings the surroundings are not natural, but artificial. In fact "man lives in two environments, the one cosmical and natural, the other economic and artificial. It is the latter which is created by human wit; the combined action and reaction of these two determining the evolution of society." In the absence of a *juste milieu* many who come off victors owe their success not to superior merit, but to greater advantages of position; the elect are not always the most select. On the contrary the struggle for existence often ends in the survival of the unfittest. The advantages of fortune and position only serve to destroy the natural qualities of those who enjoy them. Education in luxury and idleness has rather the effect of suppressing, than calling forth, emulation and the exercise of good parts which the struggle in a fair field without favour would naturally imply. Therefore, so far from being the mainspring of progress, the struggle for existence is one of the most rude and imperfect motors of development, doing more harm than good in a superior species gifted with intellect and conscience. These class differences and individual strife must be merged in the common battle of all against every natural obstacle to the universal good of man. "By means of conscious selection humanity must wrest the sceptre from Nature, and take the place of the deities it has dethroned." Such is the promised social triumph of the lords of creation, when they have come to rule in a soulless universe; the motto of the new faith is "*Ni Dieu, ni Maître*".

We have now brought before our readers the arguments of the partisans on either side. But before pronouncing judgment in the disputed relationship between Socialism and Darwinism, we may do now what is often done, before deciding important issues, in a court of justice where critical nicety is required in order to decide the true merits of the case. We may call in one or two specialists as assessors at the trial, of whose impartiality and competency there can be no doubt. W. Graham, the Professor of Jurisprudence and Political Economy at Queen's College, Belfast, may be taken as one of them. He has written a book on the " *Creed of Science, Religious, Moral, and Social*" with a concluding chapter on "Science and Socialism". He writes ably and without bias, with intelligent sympathy and in the spirit of benevolent neutrality on the relative position of the two movements now under consideration. Thus, for example, referring to the evils complained of by socialists as inseparably connected with the competitive system of industry, he remarks that competition itself is not to blame, "but the chance of uncertainty which accompanies the competitive *régime* is. Happily, however, this chance element, through the operation of various counteracting agencies, constantly on the increase, which tend to produce a solidarity in Man's fortunes, is being constantly reduced within narrower limits."

At the same time he regards competition as a necessary and permanent fact in human existence, as "the eternal means adopted by Nature, wiser than we, to perfect all the species of animals, and the human species conspicuously," and this not only in the noble forms of emulation, but even in its more ignoble features "works beneficially, and works also towards the production of the superior future society."

As to natural selection which implies competition, that, according to Professor Graham, is a process sure and unerring towards perfecting types and species. Individuals may suffer, but the race is the better for it, "thanks to the laws of beneficent heredity." Nature "blind and careless, even cruel and merciless" to the existing units, has benevolent designs towards the species. In the case of man—

"Nature, as human nature, begins to relent in her "severity. There has come a mitigation in the general "aspect of the competition struggle, as also in the conse-"quences to the conquered, now less disastrous than in "former less humane times. There is quarter given to "the vanquished in the social battle of life, as there is "in modern civilized warfare; there is even aid to the "wounded on both sides from an increase of her sympathy "and humanity."

The winners, amid the changes and chances of life, show consideration towards the losers, as some day the wheel of fortune may turn the other way. Here, too, one touch of Nature makes the whole world kin. Here, then, we have a "catharsis of sociological theory" after passing through the crucible of the higher criticism, divested from polemical exaggeration. On the one hand it avoids raising natural inequality, as it now exists, into an infallible dogma for all times, nor is it guilty on the other hand of travestying "the great law of solidarity". It admits the law of organic changes as the condition of social progress by slow modifications "from precedent to precedent", but at the same time it postulates a spiritual force, supplying the moral enthusiasms, helping to form the moral qualities necessary in any possible extension or generalization of associative and co-operative modes of industrial life. This would, undoubtedly, go far towards taking out the sting of such inequalities as now exist and lessening them imperceptibly in the course of time.

In a similar way Mr. Kidd in his work on Social Evolution, already mentioned above, whilst showing the conflict between the process of development which produces "social efficiency" at the expense of equality—for it rests on individualism and selection—with an inner conviction that this is not right on ethical grounds, shows how in these latter times it has provoked a revolt of the public conscience, and has resulted in the growth of altruistic sentiment as a corrective of the unmitigated individualism, or, as he oddly calls it, the "rationalism" of the earlier part of this century.

"It is evident," he says, "that any organization of "society with a system of rewards according to natural "ability can have no ultimate sanction in reason for all "the individuals. For as the teaching of reason undoubted-

"ly is that we are all the creatures of inheritance and
"environment, and that none of us is responsible for his
"abilities, or for the want of them, so in reason all should
"share alike. Their welfare in the present existence is just
"as important to the gifted as to the ungifted, and any
"regulation that the former should fare any worse than the
"latter must be ultimately, however we may obscure it, a
"rule of brute force pure and simple."

He sees, accordingly, in altruism a "tendency to strengthen and equip at the general expense the lower and weaker against the higher and wealthier classes of the community", and so to create an "equality of opportunity" in the economic arena which will, in this country at least, produce a peaceful and silent revolution whereby the classes and the masses may become eventually reconciled. And so far he agrees with the socialists, he assumes that to be a fact which they regard still as an aspiration.

Having given due attention to two specialists we may now proceed to our own verdict on the preceding question.

We readily grant at the outset certain points of agreement between ourselves and the representatives of socialism in this controversy, namely their emphatic claim of man's freedom from the tyranny of necessary law and the blind forces of nature, their vindication of the freedom of volition and their claims on behalf of ethics to count as a factor in the formation of social institutions and in the direction of the course of social life. At the same time we would point out that, strictly speaking, the socialistic distinction between the fatalities of nature and the fatalities of society is inadmissible from the materialistic standpoint of modern Socialism. For, regarded from that point of view, social phenomena are subject like all the rest to the impersonal laws of nature, and the evolution of social organisms transpires in accordance with those laws. It is quite true that there are artificial hindrances to the full development of some of the social units by reason of social arrangements. But we take exception to this being put entirely to the account of conscious effort for the maintenance of class privileges. They are, on the contrary, attributable in a great measure to natural inequalities in the mental and moral as well as the purely physical constitutions of social units, simply considered as "products of nature". It is a contradiction to acquit nature in one place, as the writers on the socialist side constantly do, so as to make society responsible for all inequalities and inequities, and then, again, to make appeals to an associated humanity to "subalternize nature", thus blind in the bestowal of her gifts and favours, with a view to control her vagaries by force of man's reason and will. The principle—individualistic rather than socialistic—of "*la carrière ouverte à tous les talents*," is unassailable in itself, but it is inconsistent to deny the possibility of its working on the ground of prevailing impediments in the social environment. From his own standpoint, as a monistic materialist, Lafargue has forfeited the right of speaking of two environments. A philosophy which allows of no distinction between body and mind has no right to find fault with men who follow their *natural* propensities. Everything in a purely mechanical universe is natural, and in it the triumph of mind over matter is simply a figure of speech.

However, we are in complete agreement with the nobler aspirations of socialism, when it appeals to the altruistic duty of aiding the weak, and supporting the feeble, and using superior natural abilities for the social good of the less favoured instead of turning them to account for private ends. But we must take exception to the socialist manner of applying the law of modification and variation by adaptation and heredity—Darwin's law as they call it. For socialists in speaking of this law, as a law of modifications, omit that part of the theory which serves as an important complement of it, the doctrine of "fixity of types". This is a doctrine as essential to the Darwinian hypothesis as it is opposed to the slap-dash methods of changing the social system advocated by socialism. It explains the existence of hereditary rights, and is a powerful argument in favour of an hierarchical order of society. It is opposed to revolutionary methods.

Social improvement, to be effective, must be spontaneous, moral not mechanical, by adaptation to the existing social environment rather than by organic changes in the environment itself. As in the physical so in the social world, we see both tendencies—slight variations on the one hand with the maintenance of persistent types on the other, and this is acknowledged even by Lafargue. Without such a continuity it would be absurd to talk of law, without admitting the modifying influences of human volition nothing remains but fatalistic despair or nihilistic frenzy.

Thus it will appear that the main error of socialism, throughout this controversy, is its avidity to accept the principles of materialistic science which are inimical to its pretensions, and its readiness to clutch at weapons used by its opponents, which are utterly irreconcilable with its ethical aims. The militancy of commercial competition and the correlative attitude of militant socialism spring from the same root—a struggle for the best places by means of individual and class antagonisms. The "gospel of materialistic evolution" tends to encourage in the one a thirst for material indulgences which often has the effect of developing "moral idiots", and in the other an eagerness to imitate the drastic methods of nature in social changes which may lead to social catastrophes, because the ideas of "Dynamic Sociology" are discarded in favour of a belief in the efficacy of Dynamite.

The only remedy, from our standpoint, in what threatens to become an interminable struggle of individuals and classes, is a gradual lessening of the severity of the struggle by means of human sympathy, a modification of the methods of warfare by means of ethical and religious restraints, the revival and purification of the religious sentiment founded in Reverence and Reason, which, as Mr. Kidd justly remarks, is "the central feature of human history" and all along has "constituted one of the most persistent and characteristic features of human society." The processs of selection need not for ever be carried on at the present heavy cost of sacrifice. The spectacle of all the suffering this implies makes the poetical interpreter of modern thought exclaim

> "Are God and Nature, then at strife,
>   That Nature lends such evil dreams?
> So careful of the type she seems,
>   So careless of the single life."

And others seem unable to look "behind the veil" to

> "the hands
> That reach through Nature moulding men."

It is the moulding of man according to a divine plan

which, in our opinion, must form the foundation of the "larger hope" that

> "somehow good
> Will be the final goal of all,"

when the era of conflict will be succeeded by that of more "concerted action for social ends", through the moralizing influences of religion. But such an adjustment cannot be effected by the simple working of the laws of natural affinity in an altruistic society, as the advocates of *laissez-faire* and anarchy alike maintain in demanding "individual autonomy". Nor can it be effected by the alchemy of social nostrums, but through the supernatural efforts of faith, and hope, and love. The representatives of "scientific meliorism" and "scientific socialism" look to the union of science and public spirit for the "halcyon days of man's future". Science is to supply the dry light of intellectual lucidity, and public spirit the fervent heat of the enthusiasm of humanity. By their unbiassed operation is to be brought about the "subjugation of social forces by psychic force". But can the masses of mankind be moved by mere knowledge of the physical and anatomical condition of the body-politic? Will they be propelled into activity, or reduced to acquiescence by a love of the species Homo?

"The psychic method of evolution, with its persistent "gentleness and teleological control of forces, must finally "supersede, in human society, the generic evolution of "mindless, cruel competition—the survival of the strong "and the destruction of the weak. The era of science "will be the utopian golden age; the beautiful Psyche "(the mind), now wandering aimlessly through the world,

"will in the evolution of happiness be sought out and
"cherished, and be raised to the Olympus of a new
"heaven above the sweetness of a new earth, there to
"be joined to love, and reign evermore in all true hearts
"as the genius of Socialism and the guardian of Indivi-
"duality." *

The passage is a striking one, but the story of Psyche, to which it so eloquently alludes, points to a nobler lesson. In that charming allegory the human soul personified is represented as passing through sorrow and suffering, through probation and purification, to the rarefied regions of perfect bliss. Both the ideas of the spiritual regeneration of mankind, and that of a final resurrection, which are here embodied in mythical story, are important to the solution of social life. Without the renovation of individuals from within, the regeneration of society is impossible, whilst the hope of a final restitution of all things and the conception of life as a preparatory state, enable man patiently to acquiesce in the conditions he is placed in for that purpose, and to bear the ills of life with fortitude. This will make him a more dutiful citizen of the world, a member of society more amenable to its laws, imperfect though they be. This, whilst promoting social amity and peace, would not prevent unremitting efforts being made for reducing poverty by self-sacrificing love, reforming the weak and the wicked by winning acts and healing methods; softening savage instincts and reducing by self-imposed tasks the hard lot of those who suffer, or seem to suffer, wrongfully. It would lessen by means of Christian philanthropy and the inculcation of

* "Scientific Meliorism and the Evolution of Happiness," by Jane Hume Clapperton, p. 408.

Christian principles, as far as possible, the amount of ignorance, squalor, crime, and vulgar rapacity, as well as barbarous modes of low enjoyments among poor and rich which still survive in our boasted civilization, and this in accordance with the laws of social development taught by science and religion. The safety and salvation of society, according to these, depends on the amount of self-sacrifice of which human beings are capable. The general welfare is not secured by an equal proportion of material indulgences for all, but by the earnest striving after complete self-renunciation among all. This would enable men as individuals, and human society, as a whole, to fulfil the mission assigned to them in the divine order of the universe.

CHAPTER III

MORALITIES OF SOCIALISM

> "L'humanité organisée en un mot solidaire devient à la foi le principe et la fin de la conduite morale." JEAN JAURÈS.

"WE want an order of things in which the mean and cruel passions are under complete control and all the benevolent and generous passions aroused, we want to see in this country egoism replaced by ethics, honour by honesty, and decency by a sense of duty." Such were the words of Robespierre in 1793, and ever since then it has become generally recognized that what nowadays is called the Social problem resolves itself into a question of ethics, and for the simple reason that it cannot be solved without reference to man's moral nature.

We are told, moreover, by the late founder of the *Revue Socialiste* in its March number for 1890, a writer of undoubted probity and intellectual integrity, himself called the representative of "Moral Socialism", that moral regeneration can only be expected to flow from a previous social transformation, having for its object, in the first instance, "the Solidarist organization of labour and economic Justice". Socialism, he says, distinctly wants to get rid of the subversive principle of *self-interest,* which is the inspiring motive of an iniquitous *bourgeois* society, and to substitute

for it the beneficent motives of Social interest. But
Altruistic morals, he says in the concluding words of
this article, though the sign of a moral Evolution of
Socialism, cannot become effectively the law for all until
it has moral, by which he means distributive, justice for
its substratum.

This some will call putting the cart before the horse;
socialism becomes an attempt at social reconstruction to
satisfy larger demands of distributive justice, as a preliminary step to moral and social regeneration.

George Eliot experienced a shock, we are told, when
reading for the first time in her life, and at a very tender
age, a passage in *Devereux*, which informed her "that religion
was not a requisite to moral excellence". The rank and
file of Socialists are being indoctrinated with this idea in
almost every print that is placed into their hand. Speaking of the morality of religious enthusiasts, Malon, in the
article referred to, calls them "deserters from Social duty,"
because in working out their own salvation, instead of that
of Society, they are egoists.

And, says the organ of the Social Democratic Federation, *Justice*, in an article on "Social Democracy and
Morals":

"Social Democracy is not concerned with religion or
"ethics, but with the material conditions upon which these
"are based. It proposes such changes in these conditions
"as will make a higher morality possible, where the highest
"and noblest religious instinct of humanity shall have free
"play, and robbery shall cease to live." *

We propose, in the first place, to consider the moral
conceptions of Socialism, and to show how far these

* *Justice*, May 17th 1888.

principles of "progessive morality" are influenced by the modern ideas of natural evolution, and the modern tendency to "naturalize the moral man".

In the second place, we shall discuss the demoralizing effects of some Socialist theories, as well as the methods adopted for their realization.

Last of all, we may consider what can be done to counteract the baneful influences of false moral ideals, to correct immoral tendencies, and to raise the moral tone of Society, and so help in removing every obstacle to the moral and material improvement of the people.

"*Le Socialisme est la conséquence du matérialisme, et le matérialisme est le dernier mot de la négation religieuse,*" exclaims the Abbé Winterer in one of his contributions to the history of contemporary Socialism. But this is one of those cases of mistaking consequent for antecedent often to be met with in warm discussions. Materialism, doubtless, is conducive to the spread of socialistic discontent in persons who have thrown off religious faith, but still oftener such persons abjure their early creeds because their hearts have become embittered against all existing social institutions, whilst materialistic views of life are only an afterthought. "Man is what he eats" ("Was der Mensch isst, das ist er") is a coarse way of expressing with verbal nicety the materialistic creed. But men exposed to many privations in a self-indulgent age are not apt to hunger and thirst after righteousness above their fellows. Materialistic views of life are by no means peculiar to Socialists. Such doctrines are preached from the housetops by their strongest opponents, the political economists. To take a modern instance: M. G. de Molinari, in the *Journal des Economistes*, tells us positively that the laws of political economy, like those of chemistry, are *immutable;* that the production and distribution of wealth organize themselves by virtue of *natural laws—Notre évangile se résume en ces quatre mots; Laisser faire, Laisser passer.*

But, says the Socialist, "Nature is neither moral nor intelligent."

"Just so," replies another professor of the same school of abstract political economy, from the other side of the Atlantic; "there is no injunction, *no ought*, in political economy. A Sociologist who whould attach moral applications and practical maxims to his investigations would entirely miss his proper business."

The Socialist takes him at his word, and says in return:

"We have admitted that our will itself is determined
"by natural laws.... we have acquired a more profound
"knowledge of the laws which govern social phenomena.
"We know that as our human nature is essentially capable
"of modification and perfection, so social phenomena and
"industrial phenomena, being based thereon, are modifi-
"able in a large degree, and we labour to modify them
"as much as possible—" that is, by means of such modifications which seriously affect the structure of society; in other words, social revolutions.

Again, the moral philosopher of the day, who is also a warm defender of the purely individualistic theory of Society, shows how the same laws of heredity and adaptation, which govern the phenomena of the physical world, prevail likewise in the region of social biology and moral evolution. Socialism readily accepts this "conception of man, as in his moral attributes a subject of natural science." And more than this. Having embraced a purely mechanical view of the universe, it not only rejects the belief in a superintending Deity, but proceeds also to heap ridicule on "the absurdities" of idealism in every shape and form. Thus Lafargue, son-in-law to Karl Marx, in the series of Lectures originally delivered in the *Cercle de la Bibliothèque Socialiste*, in Paris, to which we referred above, holds up to universal contempt all ideas transcending the realities of existence and the persons who were foolish enough to entertain them, whether they worship one God, or a plurality of immortal ideas, such as justice, liberty, or brotherly love.

The representatives of modern science as we have seen, in their eagerness to disown any connection between such brutal confessions of materialistic Socialism and the Darwinistic theory, take pains to show that the doctrines of selection and the survival of the fittest encourage the perpetuation of inequality, and therefore are opposed to levelling—that in fact they favour the superior privilege of minorities, and thus are essentially aristocratic, not democratic, in their tendencies. This is notably done by Häckel in the same pamphlet in which the principles of modern ethics are derived from the social instincts of the higher animals. The Socialist accepts the "ethics of science" for what they are worth. But he reminds the world that there are shorter cuts than the evolutionary process and the slow social development it implies, and that by means of physical force, as one of the forces of nature, when applied to society, great changes may be effected in less time. He shows how, according to the law of morphology in all things, the death of one form of society simply means its survival in another form, superior to that which it has rudely pushed aside in the struggle for existence.

Lastly, the ethical materialist, who has raised egoism into a dogma, and in the selfish pursuit of personal happiness in each social unit anticipates the final establishment of a harmony of interests, is confronted by the Socialist with the counter statement that, on the contrary, egoism is the last root of all evils, and its eradication the condition of morally organizing mankind.

Here we see how much of what is materialistic in the tendencies of Socialism must be in a great measure attributed to the influence of modern phases of thought in the world of science and philosophy. Every economic theory may be traced to the prevailing moral and material influences of the times. So, too, Socialism in its higher moral claims only gives expression, though in an exaggerated manner, to truths which are forcing their way to the surface among thinking people; and thus it happens that, whilst emphatically rejecting the "metaphysics of morals" and preferring to follow a moral law "enforced by purely natural sanctions", Socialists none the less take high moral ground in judging of social institutions and giving expression to their ideals of social duty.

Bearing this in mind, we may now note some of the specific charges of Socialism which have provoked and are provoking its feelings of moral indignation, together with some of its proposals for moral adjustment and the ethical discussions they give rise to.

One of the most common complaints is that of "moral atrophy" produced by long hours of labour (we omit a number of similars forming a group of grievances by itself, such as the immoral effects of the mixture of sexes in factories, the degrading influences of unhealthy dwelling-houses, and the increase of crime attributed to the uncertainty of employment owing to the conjuncture of trade and speculation). Complaining of the long hours of labour in factories, Benoit Malon, in *Le Nouvel Parti* (Vol. I. p. 88) writes thus:—

"L'exténuation a pour conséquence l'atrophie morale, "elle prépare les générations d'esclaves. Il faut, en effet, "être exceptionellement trempé pour résister, sans rien per-"dre de son energie, à des journées de douze à seize heures "de travail. Les ouvriers ainsi exténués n'ont plus la *force* "*morale* nécessaire pour travailler collectivement à l'améli-"oration de leur destinée; l'extrême fatigue du corps étouffe "leur pensée."

No one can deny the important bearings of this question on the mental, as well as the moral, development of those engaged in the centres of industry. But when we are told by the same author in the very next page what use the labourer is to make of his additional hours of leisure:—

"L'ouvrier ayant un peu de loisir pour penser, réfléchit "sur la situation; il voit qu'il est durement commandé, "indignement exploité; il cherche avec ses camarades les "moyens d'améliorer sa condition; il devient Socialiste... "La diminution des heures de travail est le moyen le plus "sûr de révolutionner la classe ouvrière, c'est à dire de la "ranger sous le drapeau Socialiste"—

we find that here we have one of those false notes in the moral tone of Socialism which obviously create strong suspicions as to the general sincerity of its moral indignation against social wrongs, and as to the genuineness of its proposals for social reform, suspicions which naturally withdraw from it the moral sympathy and support of those who possess both the power and the will to improve the position of the wage-earning classes.

However, the question as to the moral effects of long hours of labour and the like forms only part of the general question as to how to bring about a more equitable distribution of wealth, *l'égalité morale*, and how to remove the crying wrong implied in the phrase, "The rich are rich because the poor are industrious." It is not in the fitness of things, according to the moralities of Socialism, that an idle class should live in luxury and indulgence, whilst large multitudes are condemned to lifelong toil. Only in a few exceptional cases, mental and moral merit, or demerit, it is said, is the cause of these differences, and this is inexcusable on any principles of equity.

"The very idea of distributive justice, or any proportionality between success and merit, or between success and exertion, is in the present state of society so manifestly chimerical as to be relegated to the region of romance."

Such are the words of J. S. Mill in *Chapters on Socialism* published after his death in the *Fortnightly Review* in 1879.

Poverty itself, in the opinion of the modern Socialist, is an injustice, and pauper laws, iniquitous in their origin and impotent in their application, are nothing else but the acknowledgment of the injustice here complained of. It is the faulty state of society which deprives the labouring poor of the only means of earning a livelihood; whilst starvation cases in a highly civilized community are not only an anachronism, but their occurrence is an unpardonable sin in a "moralized State". Private benevolence, or delegated charity by means of public institutions is nothing else but the conscious introduction of safety-valves into the mechanism of society to prevent insurrectionary explosions—making a virtue of necessity. Spurning such doles of public benevolence, the Socialist exclaims:—

"As the individual must be just before he can be truly "generous, so must human society be based upon justice "before it can be based on benevolence." *

"Break your bread to the hungry," says a German Socialist † on this point, "help the needy in their distress, "especially where it is undeserved; but in so doing, do "not neglect the more important duty to organize the "State and society in such a manner that everyone may "find his place, so as to enable him to produce honest "and useful work and to secure for himself, with the aid "of thorough education, a dignified human existence as "the result of his labours; this is the only remedy against "pauperism."

But, it is said, the best answer to such and similar "vague schemes of sophistical Socialism" is the fact that our people "are possessed almost to a man of a *passion* for accumulation." It is forgotten that the inordinate desire for possession as a means of satisfying the cravings of insatiable luxury among the rich, at the same time excites the envy of the poor, who are too much out of tune with the "progress of the age" to join in its hymn of praise "*aurea nunc sunt saecula*". The real danger of modern society exists in this ever widening gulf between those who live in abundance and those who are in want; the passion for accumulation widens it more and more, and, as a Christian Socialist on the Continent puts it in

* H. George, *Social Problems*, p. 115.
† Frohme, *Die Entwickelung der Eigenthumsverhältnisse*, p. 130.

a few incisive words, "*le soif de l'or engendra le soif du sang.*"

The Social reformer, putting little faith in the artificial methods of equalizing wealth, remembering the demoralizing effects of a sudden rise of wages among labourers, and the vices bred by fortunes made in a day, admits, indeed, the necessity of "moralizing wealth" as well as the truth that "industry must be moralized". He will do what he can to stay the further spread of immoralities arising from material misery. He will encourage every effort to raise the standard of life, fostering at the same time a growing appreciation of higher enjoyments. But all this implies moral attainments which make human beings comparatively independent of corporeal conditions. The Socialist Bebel, on the contrary, maintains:—

"To grant to all equality in the conditions of existence, "to secure a life of human dignity for each, is the most "morally disinterested and noble measure that could be "adopted by society."

Moral dignity does not depend on the conditions of existence, *i.e.* the material conditions, and the socialist who thinks that it does descends from his high pedestal of social idealism to the level of those who scramble for material means of indulgence to heighten the enjoyment of life.*

However, the most pointed shafts of socialistic criticism are directed against the immoral tendencies of the universal system of competition, as such, apart from particular cases

* In a recent number of the *Revue Socialiste* this is explained to be an impersonal egoism, "égoisme de classe", "égoisme humain ensuite" and as such excusable, see an article by Jean Jaurès on Malon's "*Morale Sociale*" in the January number for 1894.

of social injustice and the generally imperfect social arrangements resulting from it. Competition is charged as morally responsible for every social wrong. Others, whose duty it is to guard zealously the moral health of the community, may speak with toleration and even approval of this "bloodless and not ignoble war of production and exchange." The Socialist has no words strong enough to express his disapprobation and loathing of this "natural" process of production and exchange. Calling forth, as it does, the sordid passions, such as envy and covetousness, it beguiles man into mean and monstrous acts of trade dishonesty under the mask of free contract and fair play.

Such a state of things, it is urged, does not deserve the name of social organization, and cannot be defended on ethical principles; it is anarchy, a war of individuals and classes, where the strongest or most cunning prevail, and where in every hundred human beings the ninety and nine are debased and enslaved for the benefit of the one, on the principle *Homo homini lupus*.

A society, having for its guiding principle self-interest, is engaged in a process of gradual self-destruction; the moral bonds which link together man to man in the association of equals, and still more so in the mutual relations of unequals, whose interests clash, are thereby loosened, and this must sooner or later lead to the dissolution of the social organism.

Thus, social disintegration is the consequence of a false economic theory which starts from the supposition that the common welfare is tantamount to the sum and substance of individual successes, irrespective of their ethical bearings, not only as far as the winners, but also the losers are concerned in this game of chance, called "making a fortune".

It must be owned that in this respect a higher moral instinct guides the Socialist in his vindication of the great principle of co-operative association as the only valid "law of moral life and movement in the social world".

We now pass on to a brief consideration of the immoral tendencies of Socialism in theory or application.

To begin with, there is something demoralizing in the leading idea of Socialism, which holds society, and not the individuals of which it is composed, responsible for all the evils complained of in the social system. To make social institutions responsible for crimes and misfortunes which are the accompaniments of social progress, instead of tracing them to the imperfections and vices of individuals is to sap the foundation of morality. Yet this is done by eminent Socialists past and present. Thus, *e.g.*, Louis Blanc, in his *Organisation du Travail* (p. 179) says:—

"On accuse de presque tous nos maux la conception "de la nature humaine; il faudrait en accuser le vice des "institutions sociales. Regardez autour de vous; que d'apti- "tudes déplacées, et par conséquence dépravées! Que "d'activités devenues turbulentes, faute d'avoir trouvé leur "but légitime et naturel. On force nos passions à traverser "un milieu impur, elles s'y attirent; qu'y a-t-il de surpre- "nant à cela? Qu'on place un homme sain dans une "atmosphère empestée, il y respirera la mort."

Still more emphatically says one of the most distinquished of contemporary Socialists, "Man is what society has made him;" and another, "What is designated as the act of human 'free will', is nothing else but the result of the *most powerful motives, determined by external conditions.*"

The danger of such opinions lies in the partial truth they contain; their fatal error is in their incompleteness rather than in their utter fallacy. Many evils, no doubt, are attributable to man's environment, and not a few are chargeable to economic maladjustments. But, in enlarging on them, Socialists ignore entirely the force of moral energy in opposition to the powers which drag men downwards, as well as the virtue of moral effort which potentially exists in human beings to resist temptation. It is man's fault and not his misfortune to yield feebly to immoral tendencies, or to allow, from culpable lethargy and inaction, the force of circumstances to triumph over the force of will. Such volitional delinquencies are natural enough, but natural imperfections may be corrected by moral discipline, and the punishment of men in societies for disregarding the law of compensation in the conservation of moral forces is social extinction.

This kind of moral *laissez-faire*, is worse than the principle generally understood by this phrase when referred to Governmental inaction. For to appeal to the regulating functions of the community whilst denying personal responsibility in the citizens, each by himself, amounts to the same absurdity as to expect great things from the collective wisdom of the total number of madmen in a lunatic asylum.

Every appeal to the public conscience of the nation implies some belief in the claims of private conscience; human agents without ethical responsibility, when taken separately, do not become moral in the aggregate.

The absurdity of this position, however, finds, to some

extent, its explanation in the peculiar tactics of Socialism. It demands the rectification of human affairs by the State, considered in the light of a self-regulating machine, whilst the self-regulating principle in the individual man is supposed in abeyance, for reasons not quite in keeping with the requirements of moral candour. The State is invoked to punish the malefactors of Society—malefactors, that is, in the language of Socialism, and from an economic point of view; to magnify the office of the State in this fashion is to strike a blow at Capitalism. When the legal execution has finally taken place, the executioner may be dismissed. When the State has abolished capitalism, the people will take matters into their own hands. In the same way social institutions are held responsible for the wrongs which exist in society, because this is the most powerful way of weakening the foundations on which society reposes; hence the attacks on the laws of property and calls on the State to place its sentinels at the three principal entrances of the treasure-house of national wealth —Rent, Interest, and Profit. Thus from the Socialist standpoint, "the ethical aspect of the land question" and its solution may be put in one sentence: Rent is robbery, therefore confiscate the land for the good of the people. So, too, to preserve the morality of interest, State regulation of the credit system is indispensable. Profit is beyond the pale of morality altogether; it is outlawed, because the accumulation of profit is nothing else but the absorption of other men's labour by the employer. Such forms of "exploitation" would be impossible, argues the Socialist, but for the existence of legal rights and liberties which make the unjust acquisition of property possible. Therefore what the State has given the State can take away.

It has sanctioned fraud in permitting social prerogatives and class privileges, surviving in a modified form in the monopoly of land and capital possessed by a small minority. Therefore legislation in conformity with moral law should rescind the laws which thus favour the iniquity of the existing partition. All this amounts simply to making use of the political power for attacking society in its most formidable strongholds.

There is a close connection between the institution of property and that of the family. Accordingly, Socialism directs its attacks with equal vehemence against the latter as against the former, since these two are the main props of the social order it is bent on subverting. Nothing can be more contemptuous than the tone adopted in socialistic writings when treating on the subject of "la famille autoritaire", or the institution of the family, as resting on Divine authority. The indissoluble nature of the marriage bond itself is denounced as a degrading union maintained by compulsion, although morally non-existent when the affections have been gradually alienated; or when, perhaps, disappointment, if not dislike, have taken the place of former love. Frequent violations of the domestic sanctities in "high life" are quoted as the natural consequence of this state of things. Socialists sneer at the manner in which sexual irregularities are visited by society with its "satiated virtue" and its "solvent morality", whilst the cunning and calculating spirit in which marriages in all ranks of society are contracted passes as a matter of course. Here, too, social sins are condoned on the plea that they have for their causes bad social laws, which legalize children born in wedlock, but at the same time legalize a new form of slave-trade and infanticide; since it is a notorious fact that a vast number of proletarian children become factory helots, and a still larger number of infants die of starvation or neglect, on account of the employment of mothers away from the home. From Bebel's work on woman, which has passed through no less than six editions, it would seem that the only remedy for such evils is the entire abolition of the marriage institution, whilst in the following passages we have an illustration of those immoral forms of morality which are a peculiar trait of modern thought.

"We Socialists demand a new moral state of things "in place of this kind of traffic in human flesh; we demand "that mutual attachment and moral esteem shall be the sole "bond of union between man and woman, and that all "children shall participate in the natural right of a good "education, not only those who are the legitimate children "of rich families."

"The bond of union between the sexes can only be "moral, and can be dissolved when the characters do not "harmonize. This would be, at all events, more consonant "with the principles of ethics than the peace of households "broken, which is one of the most common occurrences in "the present day."

Lastly, we have to say a word on the doubtful morality of some of the methods of force or craft which Socialism frequently adopts to propagate the cause.

Force is resorted to in the recently organized "dynamite campaign", which, it is only fair to say, is disapproved of and discountenanced by the moderate and by far the most numerous section of Socialists. This requires no further comment: it stands self-condemned morally. But no less reprehensible from an ethical point of view is the practice of concealing real intentions under false names; and yet we meet with unblushing avowals concerning the tactics adopted in electoral campaigns, and in the modes of participating in Parliamentary debates where matters of social legislation are concerned, which leave no doubt as to the ultimate object in view—namely, that of secretly paving the way for a social revolution whilst overtly engaged in the cause of social reforms. The final goal is a social *bouleversement*, and the means adopted for bringing it about are: sowing the seeds of discord in electioneering speeches and keeping up the cry of social grievances in legislative assemblies. The immorality of Socialistic opportunism, in short, consists in pushing on its forces for an impending social war whilst professedly holding a parley to arrange the preliminaries of peace, and in dishonestly masking intended attacks by conciliatory advances.

"*Political hypocrisy* has become the law of self-preservation for us social democrats," is the confession of the organ of the moderate party.

To pursue high social ideals with such methods is scarcely moral, though we are fully convinced that a high moral ideal inspires the movement as a whole. It has also to be added by way of extenuation that political repression is often the cause of political hypocrisy in the weaker opponent. Nor is political integrity the chief characteristic of the ruling classes. But two wrongs do not make one right.

We have now considered both the moralities and the immoralities of Socialism—its philosophical views of life, reflecting current phases of thought, and in its nobler aspects exhibiting a high-minded ideal of Social Morality at times in keeping with the spirit of Christian ethics. We have also glanced at some particular charges of social wrongs, arising from the general process of industry, of which they form a part, and the universal principles underlying it. Under the head of immoralities, we have noted a fatal leaning towards moral Antinomianism accompanied by an impatient opposition to those human institutions on which society is founded, and a choice of means for compassing these ends, which amount to a systematic design of destroying the social fabric. The result of our inquiry is the melancholy conviction that some of the adverse criticisms of imperfections in the present social system are founded on fact, specially when viewed from the highest moral standpoint. But we have seen at the same time a still greater incompleteness in the moral equipment of the critics, and their incapacity for the task of social reconstruction on a moral basis. This leads to the further question, What is to be done to remove the imperfections in the actual condition of things, and to raise the moral standard among all ranks of society?

First, as to the application of ethics to "business principles". "The wealth-power has been developed, while the moral and social sanctions by which that power ought to be controlled have not yet been developed," says Professor Sumner. To this retarded development of the moral consciousness in a highly advanced trading community must be attributed the excessive severity of the competition struggle, which is sometimes termed a system of commercial cannibalism, because of the apparent absence of all moral restraints—a state of things utterly at variance with the constant boasts of our modern civilization. Here, then, we see the need of the meliorating and mollifying and humanizing influences of the religion of amity to mitigate the horrors of war in the predatory state of modern industrialism. It is true "the discord of one age may be richer than the harmony of another." Still the ultimate goal of civilized humanity cannot be a constant state of conflicting antagonisms, but the reign of perfect peace.

But this, in the second place, requires a long process of moral education (not merely mental erudition), which is considered even by Socialists as the essential condition of any social changes which are to produce greater justice and happiness.

Among the lessons most needed for this purpose are some of these: that the wealth of the capitalist is a fund held in trust, to be administered for the benefit of society; that of all economic values that of human life is the highest, so that labour is not, like every other economic commodity, to be appraised by the quotations of the market, or what is worse, sacrificed at the altar of that deity which Mr. Ruskin calls the "Goddess of Get-on". The task of thus educating public opinion is assigned by a Positivist " to the oldest, the strongest, the most universal, the most beneficent of civilizing agencies, the influence of religion—religion systematically promoted by an organized body of teachers."* There is no lack of teachers; the point is to see that they teach the proper social lessons, and that before they teach they be duly qualified for the task.

And in the third place, to bring about a social regeneration, what is required is not only a more highly educated moral sense, but also a higher degree of ethical

* Paper written on behalf of the Positivist Society by Professor Beesly, and read at the Industrial Remuneration Conference, January 29th, 1885.

fervour, energy and enthusiasm to effect the great changes in the heart as well as in the life of society, for the latter is conditioned by the former. It is contrary to natural inclination to adopt new views and principles which run counter to habitual modes of thought and feeling, and to change the whole current of every day life accordingly. To overcome the natural reluctance of the will to sacrifice personal interests in obedience to the stern call of social duty, requires a powerful impulse; "*pour créer l'homme nouveau*", says one of the earlier Socialists, "*il faut l'idée religieuse*".

Culture and art, divorced from religion, cannot effect this, as is evidenced by the failure of humanism in the sixteenth and eighteenth centuries to bring about a great social transformation. Only religion can touch the deeper springs of life, adding warmth to light, and strength to beauty, moral earnestness to intellectual enlightenment and æsthetic refinement. So far, then, as the social question is an ethical question, it is incapable of solution without the close association of duty with religion. What is wanted is the religious conscience in the individual man to call out and collect together fresh reserves of moral force from the deeper depths of personal responsibility; the religious *pietas* of the home which places man "under the protection of moral purity, the daughter of heaven"; the religious sentiment, purifying and regulating the sympathetic emotions in all other human relationships; the religious bond of union which restores political virtue to corporate life and moral solidarity to every form of collective action on a larger scale.

This is denied by the modern Socialist and by some others who are not Socialists but leaders of modern thought.

All that is needed, it is said, is "*le motif moral*" to the exclusion of the religious motive—"*L'ancien motif théologique est fini*".

The present condition of Socialism, its evident weakness as a power to influence Society, even where it is strongest politically are a sufficient answer to this assertion. This serves to bring out more fully the truth that the victory over selfishness, over the coldness and hardness of heart which contracts the altruistic affections, and the conquest of self-mastery which calms the social passions, preventing dissipation of moral force by undue expenditure of heat, both depend on moral qualities which receive their inspiration from a deeper, a diviner source. The insufficiency of the ethics of egoism and the self-sufficirgness of exclusive altruism find their correction in religion, which, in a Divine synthesis, reconciles the moral antinomies—the law of self-preservation and the law of self-sacrifice for the general good. It assigns their relative position and importance to each, without sacrificing the common welfare to individual interests, and without "merging the particular in the universal good".

In the most recent and carefully reasoned utterances of Jean Jaurès, the eloquent and distinguished leader of the Socialists in the Chamber of Deputies speaks approvingly of Malon's *Morale Sociale* according to which humanity, organized in one solid, whole becomes at once the principle and end of moral conduct; and then he immediately defends the class egoism of the workers in the war with Society as a noble form of egoism, because they fight the battle for the whole human species, so that the final Evolution of morality culminates in a battle for the concrete realities of human existence. But even should it be true that "the glorification of the Proletariat is to be the glorification of Humanity, Humanity alone and entirely," we ask wherein then, consists this glory? To this we receive the vague reply that possibly a synthesis may be found in which Materialism and Idealism may merge, and perhaps M. Malon has a presentiment of this synthesis. But beyond this we know nothing at present. Until we do the Ideal here presented is not high enough for human aspiration and wants the inspiration needed to compass high moral aims.

"The Ethical progress of Society depends not on imitating the cosmic process, still less in running away from it, but combating it" says Professor Huxley in his Romanes lecture at Oxford. But the combat he refers to is not a duel between class and class in the struggle of life but an organized effort against "the tenacious and powerful enemy of selfishness". In this conflict our moral nature needs all the support it can get from a higher source than a sense of distributive justice. As "a moral movement" Socialism must be consciously, and intelligently, as now often it is unconsciously,—pursuing a higher aim than simply securing a full share in the results of material progress for every member of the Community. " Le combattant Socialiste," as M. Malon said in 1889 "a besoin de savoir qu'il travaille, souffre et lutte pour un complet renouveau du genre humain." *

* *Revue Socialiste*, Jan. 1889, p. 21. So, too, said Liebknecht at the Congress at Halle. "Does not socialism contain the highest morality: unselfishness, self-sacrifice, philanthropy?"

CHAPTER IV

PESSIMISM AND SOCIALISTIC OPTIMISM

> "Le Pessimisme progressiste, celui qui ne se contente pas de déplorer le mal mais poursuit l'amélioration morale et sociale de ce qui est, voilà la philosophie fortifiante dont nous avons besoin en cette époque troublée. C'est la nôtre."
> E. MUSEUX.

> "Ja, ich bin überzeugt, die Verwirklichung unserer letzten Ziele ist so nahe, dass wenige in dem Saale sind, die diese Tage nicht erleben werden."   BEBEL.

PESSIMISM is very much in fashion now, remarks Dr. Delon at the head of two articles on this subject in the *Revue Socialiste*, where with considerable skill and psychological insight he traces the cause of that despairing mood peculiar to modern thought in the very condition of Society, and then he tries to prescribe the social *régime* for its removal. Pessimism, he says, is a result of scepticism of the will, producing a sense of pain, and since the *réhabilitation du plaisir* is the great aim of the present age, Socialism, keeping well abreast of modern thought, includes in its programme the regulation of all the pleasures of the intelligence in the feelings and the senses, making its morality to consist wholly of the rational and positive system of the Morality of

Pleasure, *i.e.* hedonism—though from the socialist standpoint, he says, pessimism is immoral. This connects the subject of the present with that of the previous chapter. Whence then does Pessimism arise, and how is it to be got rid of? It is bred among the idle classes of ennui which itself comes of living in the lap of luxury, from hypertrophy; it arises among the poor from the opposite cause, they suffer from atrophy, from the enfeebling and depressing influences of poverty and penury. Thus the social organism suffers from plethora and anæmia at the same time, and Pessimism is nothing else but the expression of the feeling of *malaise* which these maladies produce. The pain which comes from inaction and the pain which comes from over-exertion alike impede harmonious development. Over-sensibility degenerates into the moral pessimism of the decadence, and the conquering Proletariat will kill or cure these *malades imaginaires* by the same treatment as that by which Dr. Abernethy cured his plethoric rich lady when he commanded her to leave her Bath chair and walk the length of her garden, namely by hard labour. This would have the indirect effect of lessening the excess of labour done by the Proletariat now, and so re-establish harmony in the Social body. Thus it would appear that the Socialist, as such, is an optimist as far as his own scheme and its effect on the future of society are concerned. Voltaire called life *une mauvaise plaisanterie* even in the optimistic 18th century; the Socialist of the 19th century is a dual being, a pessimist in his view of modern life as it is, an optimist in his view of the life that is to be in Utopia. Here, again, we find Socialism in accord with the spirit of the age with its Janus-face turned sadly on the past and present, and at the same time looking cheerfully into the future. Pessimism, no doubt, is a marked feature of modern thought. The republication in popular form of the works of its apostles in Germany and the actual existence of a Pessimist breviary and hymn-book as aids to the melancholy reflections and sombre meditations of its votaries in that country; the universal popularity of the recognised bards of Pessimism, singing their sad dirges abroad, and of poets and philosophers of native growth giving vent to Pessimistic views and sentiments at home, are all proofs of it. A host of novelists give expression to the same predominant note, and the daily and weekly press dwells on such themes as our "Blue Rose Melancholy" and the weariness which comes from the "Monotone in Modern Life". George Eliot, who called herself a Meliorist is really a Pessimist in the denouement of most, if not all, of her novels—most of all in the "Scenes of Clerical Life". The authors of "Mehalah" and "The Modern Antigone", Count Tolstoi in his stories which are turned into English and read with avidity, not to mention a host of others, are in essence profoundly sad; and there could not be a more signal proof than this of a Pessimistic wave passing over the modern mind at home and abroad. The voice of Cassandra was heard a few years ago from the lips of the author of "Enigmas of Life", and from the "Essays of Religion" by J. S. Mill, as well as in the more recent work of Mr. Mallock, "Is Life Worth Living?", and all three adopt a tone of despondency in their endeavour to solve the problem of life, and ask the question or suggest the inquiry whether the world is not after all the result of a great blunder, or "an act of blind folly". Pessimistic mysticism, affecting moral asceticism, the "ethics of pain", is popular in England just now;

it has become a habit of mind, which, like some intellectual epidemic, has made its appearance among us. In tracing its source we may be able to diagnose the unhealthy condition of things giving rise to it, and also to measure the height of our contemporary ideals. For the Pessimist, who complains of things as they are, has a higher ideal of what they ought to be; the facts on which he frames his hypothesis form a dark picture of the age in which he lives.

But the main reason of the prevalence of Pessimism at this time is the sense of disappointed hopes. Our boasts of progress, and the anticipations raised by believers in the "age of progress" at the beginning of this century, have been falsified by experience. We take up a brochure by a well-known Continental writer, entitled "The Disgrace of Modern Culture"; and find that one of the principal charges against the latter is that demoralization and suicide follow in its wake.

We take up an English newspaper presenting a pictorial view of the state of morals, with diagrams to show the rise and fall of the greater and lesser forms of crime and offences against the law, and we find a sad tale told of the evils consequent on "the high tension of modern life". In skimming over an article on the "Pessimist View of Work", in the *Spectator*, we find the growth of Socialism attributed to the social discontent "with toil as the permanent condition of existence", aggravated and abetted by the oversensitive sympathy of the labourer's friends, indulgence in pity being a special note of our modern life. It is the contrast between the Utopian dreams of a hundred years ago and the reality of to-day that has engendered desponding views of life and mind in the present.

In a long and weary uphill journey, or in a tedious sea-voyage, there are times of rest and retrospect which often lead to sad reflections. The traveller, like the three Englishmen in Mr. Haggard's story of "King Solomon's Mines", begins to doubt whether the amount of toil and patience required to reach the ultimate goal of our journey is not too high a price paid for the actual attainment. The system being lowered by fatigue, and the judgment warped by anticipatory disappointment, there follows a morbid condition of mind which is really the outcome of physical exhaustion. It is the same with whole bodies of men at given resting points of human history. A reaction sets in after a season of exciting activity accompanied by great effort and expectation, when, as the result of growing luxury and material indulgence, there follows a season of uneasy craving for more on the part of the fortunate among whom satiety has produced insatiable desire, and of disappointment among the unfortunate in proportion to the vastness of the promises which have remained unfulfilled; and this produces weary disinclination to go on. Some mere lookers-on catch this pessimistic temper by sympathy. Thus, over-refined and artistic minds, like John Ruskin, deplore the loss of taste for the beautiful in the pursuit of practical ends in these days of steam and factories. Others, like Thomas Carlyle, watching with a reformer's kindling wrath the process of materialistic degradation and moral disintegration, speak in a pessimistic vein, protesting against the actual state of things, and uttering sad and surly vaticinations in "Latter-Day Pamphlets". Poets who, like Tennyson, in their youth proclaimed the glories of progress, say, as he does, in their old age "Progress halts with palsied feet", and even the men of culture are apt to say with Mark Pattison "I am growing brooding, melancholy, taciturn and wholly pessimist." People feel unable to relapse into ease and relaxation, nor are they willing to push on with the old belief in the possibilities of the future.

Hence the alarming increase of modern Buddhists weary of life, whose philosophy is contained in the lines:

> The aching craze to live ends, and life glides—
> Lifeless—to nameless quiet, nameless joy,
> Blessed Nirvana—sinless, stirless rest—
> That change which never changes.*

The poets and philosophers are the best exponents of contemporary thought and life. They reflect the age they live in, though, no doubt, their inmost thoughts and personal experiences colour the tincture of their writings. The poets especially "teach in song" "what they have learned in sorrow." There are those who, like Sir John Lubbock in the charming volumes on the "Pleasures of Life", try to make the best of things, but even he in speaking of the joys of life does so avowedly to counterbalance his melancholy thoughts.

Of the three illusions which von Hartmann tries to dispel, one is the hope of social happiness, and yet in order to sweeten the cup of bitterness to our fellow-mortals, he recommends social amelioration as a matter of duty. If it were true, as a Socialist admirer of Schopenhauer wrote on the last page of a memoir of that

* "The Light of Asia; or, The Great Renunciation," by Edwin Arnold C.S.I., Book VI. In this work the pessimistic creed of Eastern and Western mysticism combined are beautifully reflected.

writer, published two or three years ago, that social conditions determine the fate of humanity, then, indeed, with the removal of the causes we would remove human misery, and with it put an end to Pessimism itself as a philosophy of human life. But, since we are told that Pessimism is a "scepticism of the will" the motor force is wanting here for great efforts to improve society. Egoism, ill-will, and pity are the three chief motors prompting human action, according to Schopenhauer. Are these sufficient for the purpose?

Pessimism is an excellent system of social pathology; it fails as a system of therapeutics. It is full

> Of pity for the sickness of this world,

but its pity is accompanied by the Social passion which would kill the patient outright. Pessimism, in its merciless diagnosis of human suffering and guilt, sees only the evil in man's present existence, and in so doing, when it does not exaggerate, holds up the mirror to an age given to self-laudation. It wants to put an end to "the world's process". Here Socialism and Pessimism coincide. The theory of Karl Marx ends in the death of Society. According to him things must grow worse and worse in the course of Capitalistic development until the antagonism of classes has reached the acute stage. Then follows the liquidation of Society. But suppose this to have taken place and social democracy to be triumphant, if the pessimistic theory of life is true we are yet a long way off the millenium—for, according to the theory of von Hartmann, the Social ideal is an illusion and the Socialist Commonwealth would be an illustration of it.

But Socialists are sincerely pessimistic only in their

criticism of the present state of society and their prophetic utterances on its fate. As soon as they come to speak of the Commonwealth they purpose founding on its ruins they become optimists immediately. As far as they are sincere pessimists, however, they are right, and their criticism is useful in pointing to some of the fallacies of a "sated Optimism" which would leave things as they actually are in this best of social worlds, according to the most recent expressions of "Evolutionary Optimism", such *e.g.* as Camille Dreyfus, whose work on "l'Evolution des Mondes et des Sociétiés" is simply an elaboration of the dictum "*L'Evolution est fatale, ininterrompue et progressive.*" The faith of such believers in the "social happiness" principle under existing circumstances may be briefly stated thus: There is a way of harmonizing the best interests of the individual with social development in the fulfilment of social duty, and there is no greater happiness than the bliss of dutiful obedience to social laws, including "the joy of dutiful renunciation". This is the modern version of utilitarian opportunism, "the greatest happiness of the greatest number," as modified by the recent teachings of social ethics. This optimistic creed has been in vogue ever since the days of Adam Smith, and has been of late ably restated in Mr. Crozier's volume on *Civilization and Progress*, closing with a full belief in the future, when

"Science, by diving into the deep elements of the "problem—material and social—and ascertaining the physi- "cal and spiritual laws on which it depends, will, by "again enabling us to *equalize* the conditions, prepare the "way for a new and higher social *régime* than any that "history has yet recorded."

Similar, and resting on similar grounds, were the hopes of the Economists at the close of the last century, believing with Adam Smith in "the natural progress of opulence", depending "on the natural effort of every individual to better his own condition when suffered to exert himself with freedom and security." But there is this difference, that a social problem now stares us in the face which did not then exist, or even was dreamt of, but has been evolved from the very conditions here described, *i.e.* unlimited individual liberty and expansion.

We, therefore, are often now invited to put our faith in "the gradual *amelioration* of the material and social conditions of men", since the "evolution of happiness" is made contingent on "scientific meliorism". Economic optimism, therefore, to be complete, must take in the future as well as the present, and therefore, as far as the present is concerned, it is not and, as we shall show, cannot be a whole-hearted optimism, in spite of the cheerful assurances of the crowd of *laudatores temporis acti* who have not sufficient penetration or integrity of mind to perceive this. But even a hasty glance at the optimistic literature of the Jubilee year is sufficient to show this. For even those writers who were selected for the task of giving a "survey of fifty years' progress", on account of their optimistic proclivities, tell us that it affords matter of serious reflection, warning us to be sober-minded in reviewing our past achievements, whilst we are none the less thankful for what advance has been made in more than one direction. Mechanical inventions for saving labour and a marvellous development of industrial machinery have vastly increased material wealth, but, as the late Professor Leone Levi reminds his readers whilst presenting them with a glowing picture of growing prosperity, it "is by no means all gold that glitters in our economic system."*

According to the laws of "superorganic evolution"—the so-called natural laws of political economy which the physiocrats of a hundred years ago promulgated in France—all that is required was stated to be this: Let each man try to improve his own condition, "*et le monde alors va de lui-même.*" Therefore "*laissez faire, laissez aller;*" and all will go well. The principle has been tried for a century, with what results? The doctrine of "*laissez faire*" is discredited on all hands, and its opponents argue as follows: The number of millionaires has been increased with the means of amassing mountains of gold, but with "a new race of manufacturing plutocrats, rising and falling like so many golden sandhills", there has risen up in all civilized and progressive countries a vast multitude of miserable starvelings, scarcely able to eke out bare existence, and among the mechanical discoveries of the age are not only machines which make mind unnecessary and manual labour cheap, but also "infernal machines", the invention of dynamite engines being one of the latest results of "this age of progress", intended in their way to hasten on the "social improvement of the masses". The marvellous growth of cities is accompanied by the evils of over-crowding and the dull depression of de-

---

* "The Material Growth of the United Kingdom from 1836 to 1886," by Prof. Leone Levi, *Fortnightly Review*, June, 1887, p. 914. In Mr. Giffen's latest utterance on the "Recent Rate of Material Progress in England" and Prof. Levi's lecture in King's College on the "Progress of Commerce and Industry," both writers speak in a still more subdued tone of plutocratic optimism. See *Times*, September 2, 1887, and October 14, 1887.

populated country districts. The minute division of labour in the centres of industry is accompanied by the concentration of the proletariat, drilled in factories and trained by agitators for common action against those whom their toil has enriched, whilst even "subsistence wages" are rendered precarious by the commercial fluctuations and consequent oscillations in the labour market, so as to render the basis of society in its lower layers ominously insecure.

These are some of the "matters which may be fairly grouped under *that debatable word progress*"—so debatable that some even speak of it as an "advance backwards". We are not of this number; still the matter wears a serious aspect for would-be optimists.

Voltaire, in his *Candide*, referred to the earthquake of Lisbon to point out the flaws in the materialistic optimism of his own times. Sceptics nowadays might point to those social earthquakes in diverse places, of which we hear so much now, as symptomatic of volcanic forces of social discontent underground, and as facts which cannot be reconciled with a profession of economic optimism. Leibnitz, optimist as he was, believed that the age he lived in was the old age of the world, and the bright future he predicted was the glow of sunset rather than of the rising dawn. Our modern optimists, so far from discovering any symptoms of senile decrepitude around them, believe, on the contrary, that we have only arrived at the earlier stage of social evolution, that existing social phenomena are only the beginnings of a "fuller industrial and social development". A change of tenses is enough to distinguish the optimism of the nineteenth from that of the eighteenth century. Thus Pope said and the world tried hard to believe, that "whatever is, is right". Now we are told, "whatever is, is well; but nothing really is which is not in progressive and *militant* movement". But "militant movement" is the very phrase which suggests the difficulty which our modern prophets of smooth things have to get over, and sometimes try to gloss over, and not always very successfully. For what is called the social movement is nothing else but the "militant movement" of a certain class to gain the necessary advantages in order to its own higher social development, that class being the most numerous and able by force of numbers to give effect to its demands at the ballot-box. This is the social problem— How to reconcile the rise of democracy with social conditions resting on aristocratic institutions. This is the great question which taxes the ingenuity of the politician and the political economist alike, the one accentuating the functions of government in social legislation, the other accepting the forces of social life as such to work out in the natural course of things a social evolution. Both progressive statesmen and economists demand nothing else but "the elevation and expansion of the individual"; but individual expansion may, in its centrifugal effects, endanger the "symmetry and stability of society"; it may produce a revolution; and so Karl Marx and his school predict the social revolution from the effects of this actual "expansion" of individual liberties and from the reign of competition since the outbreak of the French Revolution, which rendered all equal in the eyes of the law, but has, by reason of unlimited competition, brought about greater inequalities, less bearable than ever in the "age of reason" and universal liberty. In the bursting of social bonds and setting free of individual effort, the revolution at the close of the eighteenth century began—while that at the close of the nineteenth it tries to finish—the emancipation of the masses, or the fourth estate. But, we repeat, when the social revolution is effected we have by no means reached the end of all perfection. Whilst, therefore, we agree with Socialists in their general criticism of the social system we have our own misgivings as to the correctness of their optimistic views of the future of society under their own government. The ethical optimism of Socialists rests in an implicit belief in the perfectibility of human nature. But if the highest moral level is reached in socialist ideals, in the material paradise sketched by the writers in socialist organs like those quoted in the last chapter and elsewhere in this volume, it is hard to believe in this new panacea of happiness. It is a sensible remark of Malon's that our wisdom consists perhaps in thinking *en Pessimiste*, for the nature of things is cruel and sad, and to act *en Optimiste*, for human intervention is efficacious for moral and social improvement, and that every effort of justice and kindness must be best, appearances notwithstanding. Still, it is not a philosophical answer to pessimists who sneer at the optimistic illusions of social reformers as a body; and in the long run the priciple will not work to think in one way and to act in another, for thought directs action consciously or unconsciously. We are, therefore, inclined to take up a position midway between these two extremes. Meliorism in matters social is all that can be expected. We need not despair entirely nor expect too much of human nature, but social improvement may be possible where complete satisfaction is out of the question. In this sense of the word George Eliot refused to be called an optimist, because it savoured of presumption to make one's subjective ideal world the arbitrary standard of all worlds known and unknown. But she acknowledged herself to be a meliorist, discarding the use of superlatives where comparison is so difficult, and without predicting absolute results from present effects, only professing to do what lay in her power to bring about relative improvement, and so leaving the world comparatively better than she found it. Hence the use of the term "Scientific Meliorism". Meliorism in part admits of a theory of the universe to all intents and purposes pessimistic, but recommends a practice founded on this theory so as to render a state of things in which evil predominates over good more tolerable if possible, so as to turn the balance in relieving the necessities and remedying the ills of life as far as this can be done by human agency; and, moreover, to do so in accordance with the laws of nature ascertained by science, irrespective of any speculation as to a future state of existence. It is expressed in the beautiful lines of the Spanish Gipsy.

> But if I cannot plant resolve in hope,
>   It will stand firm on certainty of woe—
> I choose the ill that is most like to end
>   With my poor being. Hopes have precarious life;
> They are oft blighted, withered, snapped, sheared off
>   In vigorous growth, and turned to rottenness.
> But faithfulness can feed on suffering,
>   And knows no disappointment.

This idea Miss Clapperton, a friend and pupil of George Eliot, has expounded in her work on "Scientific Meliorism"; in doing so she takes her standpoint on the Scientific Acquisition of the 19th century, and applies the doctrine of Evolution. As she says in the preface of her book:

"The possibility of evolving superior social conditions is,
"to my mind, a scientific certainty dependent on psychic
"effort" (p. xl). "The nineteenth century stands, I believe,
"on the threshold of a new form of social life, and on the
"eve of a new departure.... My aim is practical. By
"the study of evolution I think it possible to guide the
"thoughtful and earnest in our midst to personal conduct
"which will tend to bring about a happier social state"
(p. 49).

To the evolutionist who combines the power of "intellectual clearness" with "emotional beneficence" nothing is impossible. A lucid apprehension of the social forces at work and their causes and antecedents, together with a ready will and the wisdom which comes from knowledge to direct and extend them—in other words, "science and public spirit"—will enable him to hasten on the "halcyon days of man's future." The things to be done immediately for the moral and material elevation of the masses are briefly stated as follows, on p. 64 :—

"A gradual rise of the labourers' wages; a steady
"lowering of the prices of necessary commodities until they
"almost reach the cost of production; the gradual change
"from the competitive and capitalistic system to co-operative
"methods of production; the narrowing of hours of labour
"until time is left for daily recreation; the growth and
"spread of rational opinions concerning population, parental
"health, and parental duty, with the strengthening of all
"family ties; the opening of facilities for life insurance
"and for aiding personal efforts in accumulating wealth,
"proportional to desire, on national security; and, lastly,
"education based upon the principle that the habits, dis-
"positions, and sentiments of children have to be formed

"*for* them, and that all education must bear upon, and "lead up to, the right conduct of life."

The successive steps towards bringing all this about are as succinctly stated on p. 140 in the following "order of evolution":—

"These are, first, that in this sphere of feeling the path "of advance toward greater happiness lies in fostering the "sympathetic and repressing the anti-social emotions; "second, that the love of property must be modified and "subjected to reason; third, that jealousy is anti-social and "must die out; that love of truth and the sentiment of "justice are of recent growth, and demand general atten-"tion and aid in their development; and fifth, that the "sentiment of what is proper and improper in conventional "society is no true guide to right conduct."

All this is to be effected by individual effort of enlightened human beings in the spirit of philanthropic co-operation. Our author agrees with von Hartmann in believing that hitherto the social organism has been guided by blind impulses. But a new era is dawning on us now, "the era of self-consciousness" (pp. 117—119). The reign of the "all-wise unconscious" thus comes to an end, and conscious human will takes up the *rôle* of conducting man to his high destiny. By the "inventive interference" of the human intellect, which is "*an enormous cosmic force*" in the universe, "human evolution advances towards a perfected state determined by pure ethics! This is "the "law of the *elimination of evil, i.e.* under *the spur of* "*pain, discomfort, and injustice, it is impossible that man's* "*endeavours should cease until every preventible evil of human* "*life is overcome*" (the italics are the author's) pp. 395—6. For a full enumeration of all the good which follows upon this final extirpation of evil we must refer our readers to the book itself, and the chapter entitled "Scientific Meliorism", commencing p. 425. Here, too, a large demand is made on our belief in the possibilities of moral as antecedent to social evolution. The development of altruistic sentiment which is to mitigate the evil complained of in our "individualist civilization" must be accepted as a foregone conclusion, whilst Pessimism despairs of reforming society and only believes in that evolutionary process, which, whilst intensifying continuous suffering, tends with the further development of culture to bring about the "deliverance of the absolute from his transcendental misery, "by means of the imminent torment of the world's Evo-"lution." *

In the mean time, however, even von Hartmann, in one of those self-revelations to which he seems much addicted, says of his philosophy, in comparison with that of Schopenhauer:—

"My view of the world is serious and severe, even "tragical in its conception, but by no means melancholy, "bitter, and desponding. In it, as in every tragedy, "there is a dull background in perspective, but there are "not wanting the bright tinted colours of the foreground of "the picture standing out against the dark shadows. In "it the prominent feature is the yearning after peace, "which is peculiar to every human heart capable of deep "feeling, but it directs the individual longing for it to the "grave, and the universal soul longing after it to be satis-"fied in the dim distance of the last day. At the same

* *Philosophie des Unbewussten*, pp. 396—7; and ib. 375—90, on the third stage of Illusion—the Illusion of Scientific Meliorism to affect human happiness socially.

"time it discourages any inclination to weariness among
"those who work in the daytime as premature and un-
"becoming, as only suitable to the season of rest. It has
"its roots in all the ramifications of manly energy, creative
"effort, vigour of action; it is thus far on the side of
"historical activity as understood among the moderns and
"in the West, as distinguished from the passivity of the
"East, especially among the Hindoos. Its conception of the
"misery and unspeakable wretchedness of life is sharply drawn,
"and with no attempt to gloss them over. But the know-
"ledge so obtained is to serve only as a spur to redoubled
"energy, and it is utterly opposed to the womanish and
"feeble sentimentality which broods over the world's
"sorrow, and never gets further than passive sympathy,
"but is rather apt to luxuriate in the over-sensitive emo-
"tionalism of its lamentations, and the sickliness of its
"hyperæsthetic sensibility."

Still, without some faith in the potentiality of moral progress attempts at social amelioration, however nobly conceived, would scarcely be effectively maintained. Moreover, as Mr. Kidd in his work on Social Evolution has shown, "the great process *is* proceeding as a natural and orderly development", a sa matter of fact, and side by side of it the growth of the altruistic sentiment on which such hopes are built, and, as the same writer shows:—

"It is in this softening of the character, in this deepening
"and strengthening of the altruistic feelings, with the in-
"creased sensitiveness to stimulus, and the consequent
"ever-growing sense of responsibility to each other, that we
"have the explanation of all the social and political move-
"ments which are characteristic of the period."

Whether from this a pacification of society may be

expected and a new start given to social progress without its drawbacks is another question. When Comte wrote his "General View of Positivism" in 1848 he thought he had discovered this fundamental principle in Positivism, that social synthesis was to be brought about by the final victory of social over selfish affections; that real happiness was to be found at last in "the highest possible development of the social instincts", that the "complete organization of moral force was reserved for modern times", and that this progress in morality would end in the subjection of self-interest to social feeling and the substitution of moral for political agencies in the renovation of society. Thus Positivism steps in to regenerate society on a scientific basis of sociology. We are still waiting for the great transformation which Comte expected from a wider conception of his own views.

It suggests the question whether all previous attempts to solve the social problem antecedent to the rise of the Positivist Philosophy having failed, the latter is destined to face it with a greater measure of success so as to save the world from Social Pessimism? This is the subject reserved for our consideration in the next chapter.

CHAPTER V

SOCIALISM AND POSITIVISM

> "We here have very real affinities and sympathies with Socialism, and are wont to describe Positivism as a form of moral and religious socialism. But we have very distinctly insisted on the moral and social value of the personal appropriation of capital, the indispensable need of the capitalist as a normal institution, and the equal need of moral and religious control over the use of capital as essential to civilization."   FREDERIC HARRISON.
> *New Year's Address 1895.*

"SOCIALISM is pessimistic in so far as it says that things cannot be worse than they are now, and optimistic in declaring, like Positivism, the ultimate perfectibility of man in a social state which is the only panacea for all Social Evils." So wrote an idealist in *To-Day*, in 1886. This shows the connection between the subject of the last chapter and this. Comte, indeed, was not altogether an Optimist; on the contrary he dwells upon the fact that the arrangements of the universe are far from being such as to ensure human happiness, and that it is only by man's own "providential action" in conquering natural obstacles by scientific knowledge and its application, and by following the dictates of his heart and the adopting ameliorative measures and improving the social condition of his fellows that he is able to promote social happiness—that is, so far as the fatalities of Nature will let him. For in everything he must follow the rigid laws of natural development. Nevertheless it is true that in the main Positivism as a social creed, and the Religion of Humanity in supplying a creative force, aim at no less than a re-organization of the civilized world by bringing into correlation man's intellectual faculties and social sympathies and thus constructing ultimately a more perfect system of society. Thus "Sociology" which is "the crowning effort of the Positivist Philosophy" in its mental and moral aspects is the Science and Art of compassing their ends — "The great object which Positivism sets before us individually and socially, is the endeavour to become more perfect" says Comte in the *General View of Positivism,* which formed part of the first Volume of his treatise on Positive Polity and which appeared in the year of the Social Democratic Revolution in 1848. It is in allusion to this movement that Comte expresses his conviction that "Positivism is the only system which can supersede the various subversive schemes that are growing every day more dangerous to all relations of domestic and social life." The questions before us are simply these: What is the character of this new Philosophy in relation to socialistic attempts to bring about the main object? How far has it succeeded as a Social Polity in gaining over the Classes and Masses to its side? What is the difference in principle and method between Positivism and Socialism as two rival schemes each attempting to take the lead of the working-classes and to re-construct Society as a whole?—The ruling principle of Comte's theory is Social sympathy expressing itself in altruism, the enemy of self-seeking and as such it becomes the primal force in the re-construction of the social edifice. Intellect becomes the servant of the affections and individualistic rationalism must be displaced by the Religion of Amity; "no calculation of self-interest can rival this social instinct". The heart suggests, and the head solves, at its bidding, the social problem. It is the mind of man which grasps the idea of the material order of things, "the immutable necessity of this external world". On this objective basis of positive scientific knowledge Comtism rears its scheme of the social world and conquers nature in obedience to her ascertained laws. Positive Science and imaginative or idealizing Art serve one great purpose only, and that is the perfection of the social life of man. The universe is to be studied not for its own sake but for the sake of man, or rather Humanity. Mental discipline itself becomes a means for the better study of "the general conditions of modern Society". Thus Positivism, with "Love for its principle, order for its basis, and progress for its end", wants to reform our political institutions by a "complete re-organisation of opinion and of life", retaining what is good in the old order, marching with the vanguard of progress, having the enthusiasm of Humanity for its motive power, while the order of society rests necessarily on the natural order of the laws of the Universe. But this also includes the germ and purpose of progress. So far, therefore, as Communism implies a progress, moral rather than intellectual, it is "the natural progress in the right direction of the revolutionary spirit," because it demands a preponderance of social feeling over self-love. But since it tries to compass its views by a mechanical treatment of society it runs counter to the principle of Positivism which puts moral before political change. Even the Commune of Paris promised "a new positive experimental and Scientific Era", and its aim to found a number of federative republics was consonant with Positivist principles, though its political and revolutionary character was opposed to the latter; and for this reason the sympathies of Comtism were in the end withdrawn from the movement. It is among the working-classes that the system seeks its adherents because "they are all united by strong social instincts", and "have the largest stock of good sense and good feeling", and all that is required to give direction to their noble aspirations is systematic culture which Positivism is ready to supply. But it denies the doctrine of the "sovereignty of the people", for the natural leaders of the people are the philosophers to guide the head, and captains of Industry, a new order of chivalry to be created,—here Comte and Carlyle are at one—to guide the hand; and then "the people will gradually find that the solution of the great problem which Positivism offers is better than the Communistic solution". It does not object to the principle of Property and Inheritance. "Property is in its nature social", but it needs control, and inheritance is the natural means of transmitting the result of labour from one generation to another and thus maintaining the continuity of the social organism. The notion of Equality is anti-social, and socialistic schemes, subversive of the social order, end in a chimera. Yet Positivism agrees in this with Socialism that in the words of Comte "*La richesse est sociale dans sa source et doit l'être ainsi dans son application*". But it is opposed to Socialism because the latter starts with the idea of individual rights when it ought to begin with reciprocal duties, because it aims at mechanical instead of moral transformation, and because it rejects social reform in favour of revolution. The solution of the problem consists in "regarding our political and social actions as the service of humanity", not the subversing of the interests of this or that class. Individuals should be regarded as "organs of one Supreme Being", *i.e.* Humanity, and Capitalists and Labourers alike as public functionaries, the former performing the "nutritive functions of Humanity", the latter representing "the activity of the Supreme Being". The Positivist agrees with, and even goes beyond, the Socialist in his opposition to Egoism and Individualism when Comte declares that "*the only real life is the collective life of the race; that individual life has no existence except in an abstraction*". But Positivism would not destroy Individualism, but only make it subserve the welfare of the community. It is by means of the spiritual leaders, the philosophers or the high Priests of Humanity who perform its cerebral functions and assume the spiritual government, that the populace and the rest will be taught this supreme social doctrine; and the scientific training purposed by Positivism will finally produce the social spirit which will animate society and peacefully work out its salvation. As a provisional measure the holder of dictatorial power should be chosen from the working-classes, since, indeed, "the Proletariat forms the principal basis of the social system. And since love of man for man is the living principle of social action, woman's influence, especially in the family, is of paramount importance, feeling, reason, activity corresponding to the three elements of the regenerative movement, Women, Philosophers, and People." Art, which the revolutionary spirit discourages, is re-introduced by Positivism into the modern social system for the purpose of strengthening our sympathies and in it the unity of human nature finds its representative. From this point of view Utopias, as the product of the æsthetic genius of Humanity, have helped in idealizing the facts of social life, they are the poetry of politics. Thus the culture of Art becomes a moral force in Society. But Science, Art, and Morality, are all devoted to the service of Humanity, "the new great Being", as "the life of the individual is in every respect subordinate to the Evolution of the race", and to live in others is in the truest sense life. The superiority of Positivism as a religion over Christianity consists in this impersonal notion of living entirely for others; social not personal bliss is its object, since for the love of a personal God it substitutes the love for Humanity, and to be incorporated into this "supreme being" at last is its only and unselfish hope. This puts an end to the conflict between Creed and Science, the revolt of the intellect against the heart, rationalism and religion, independence and social union, in the Positivist scheme, for it places "the foundation of social science on the basis of the preliminary sciences", making Humanity the sole object of worship and work.

The work Positivism sets itself to do, according to Comte's *Catechism of Positivism*, is "to deliver the West from anarchical democracy, and from retrograde aristocracy, so as to constitute, as far as practicable, a true Sociocracy, one combining wisely, in furtherance of the common regeneration, all the powers of man, each in every case brought to bear according to its nature". And this social polity rests on the foundation of a new religion which is defined in the same catechism as "the state of perfect *unity*, which is distinctive of our existence, both individual and social, where all its parts, moral and physical, habitually converge towards a common purpose. This definition of Religion delineates, then, the unchanging type to which tends more and more the totality of human effort. Our happiness and our merit consist, above all, in drawing as near as possible to this Unity, the gradual development of which is the best measure of real progress towards individual and social perfection".

We may, in the next place, enquire how far these views are shared by the most recent exponents of Positivism in England, and what steps are taken to give them effect, and also to what extent they have taken root in modern thought. Mr. Frederic Harrison in his address, entitled *A New Era*, delivered before the Manchester Positivist Society in the year of the centenary of the French Revolution, puts very clearly the standpoint of the English Positivists. That Era, he says, means "the definite substitution of scientific knowledge for obsolete fragments, of human well-being on this earth for imaginary hopes of individual bliss in heaven, of Humanity in place of self, or country, or supposed Creator, and of the faith of human progress in lieu of celestial rewards of the separate soul". To Positivists the religion of Humanity supplies the vacant place of their lost faith in Christianity; they find in it a reconciliation of Science and Religion, materialistic Atheism more or less veiled having no attraction for them. With Comte they consider the advent of the social revolution as the second stage of the political one, both resulting from the anarchical state of mind and society following upon the break-up of the feudal and ecclesiastical system and the triumph of Protestant Reformation succeeded by the French Revolution. This, they aver, has had the effect of loosening the social bonds, and by the encouragement given to critical scepticism laming the moral sinews of modern society, which nothing can restore except a new faith strong enough to produce an ethical and, by means thereof, a social regeneration, *i.e.* a firm belief in the "divinity of the human race". And this faith makes a large demand on duty towards the "vast organic being of Humanity". In the fulfilment of this will be realized the "ideal of an industrial Republic pursued for the last 100 years, which implies the formal incorporation into the highest privileges of the citizen of the entire body of the toiling masses", the extinction of privilege in every form and the recognition of the new principle of social order, which demands "the participation of the people in securing the welfare of the Commonwealth". We are here quoting from the New Year's address 1890 entitled "The Industrial Republic", where, too, we are told that in order to bring about this, Socialism is not sufficiently strong without the aid of Religion in its conflict with Capitalism, which rests on material force, and that, therefore in the Positivist solution of the industrial question lies the only complete, consistent and practical Socialism, a socialism which finds in the family the foundation of society, which cares as much for personal freedom and domestic responsibility as it cares for social combination, which sees in the personal appropriation of capital in the hands of responsible men the only guarantee of efficient production". In short, as Mr. Harrison showed in a subsequent address (1891) on "Moral and Religious Socialism", Positivism is in a large and true sense organised socialism, but with a difference, it is a moral not a material, a religious not a secular, movement, it is "a socialism founded on social science and inspired by religion, it rests on social duty not on the rights of all to the material productions of society. Therefore the task of the future, for the next 100 years, is "the incorporation of the Proletariat into society, the admission of the mass of labourers to all the advantages which civilization offers now to a select number only." Thus "the majestic march of the Human Providence" ends in the final emancipation of the workers without the enslavement of all implied in the establishment of the socialistic state and the organization of labour under its *régime*. Dr. Congreve, who represents in this country the older branch of English Positivists which insists on putting into practice the entire scheme of Comte "textually, literally, bodily, and immediately", whereas that to which Mr. Harrison belongs adopts the religion of Humanity in a more tentative and experimental way, "using the scheme of Comte as an ideal to work out and not as a Bible to obey",—agrees in the points discussed here with Mr. Harrison. Speaking in his annual address delivered at the Church of Humanity in 1890 on the progress of Socialism and its impatience and premature solutions of the social problem, Dr. Congreve says: "We conceive moral answers to be the ultimate and only answers, and re-arrangements of material interests to be quite inadequate". It is a new, a social, and moral view of labour, of industry in general—that is the real requisite in the intellectual direction, not a mechanical rearrangement of society—and again a new religion is wanted in order to produce that inner change which must precede the external rearrangement of the social order; a new Church like the medieval with power to educate, civilize, humanise, and socialise the new industrial republic, but professing a "creed capable of scientific proof".

When we turn to the practical programme in which the Positivists give effect to their social theory there is nothing in which it differs much from the social efforts of other religious denominations and philanthropic bodies. Starting from the postulate that the organized formation of our moral power is the first condition of all healthy social life, it proceeds to enumerate the following under the head of practical measures to be aimed at, namely the reorganization of the homes of the workers, sanitation, intellectual and artistic advantages to be secured to "principal centres", the immediate introduction of the eight hours' labour day, exemption of women and children from excessive and injurious labour, public holidays once a month, the institution of clubs for social and political discussion, national education, regulation of the licensing system, acquisition by the state for public use of artistic, scientific or literary treasures now in private hands, reorganization of the public services, transference of roads, railways, harbours, &c. to the State, and, lastly, the removal of the evils of poor relief and with it the abrogation of the right of state relief.* Such was the Positivist programme in 1892, re-stated in 1894. Mr. Harrison points out the revolution in the public mind during the interval. When first proposed these reforms were identified with the dreams and fads of Socialism, but they have become now the common-places of the Progressive Party and the Social Reformer. But we doubt whether the deduction drawn from this fact is correct, that the change of opinion is due to the spread of Positivist opinion; it is due rather

* Abridged from "Suggestions for practical social movement from the Positivist's point of view" contained in an article by F. Harrison on "Our Social Programme" in the *Positivist Review* of January 1894.

to the general onward move towards social reform, though it is only just to admit that the formation of public opinion on this head owes much to the Positivist thinkers, not so much because of their peculiar religious or philosophical tenets as on account of the superior intellectual power and personal worth of the men who profess them. This is especially true of Professor Beesly, whose steady light—less brilliant, perhaps, than that of F. Harrison, and less warm in its spiritual intensity than that of Dr. Congreve—sheds its rays on the social problem with an effective though altogether unobtrusive luminosity. His annual address of 1894, contained in the February number of the *Positivist Review,* states clearly and succinctly the difference between the Socialist and Positivist stand-point. "Socialists propose to effect this",—*i.e.* to vest the power of governing Industry and the country generally in the same hands—"by transferring the instruments of production from the present possessors to the existing political government, that is to the nominees of universal suffrage. Positivists would transfer the functions of political government from the nominees of universal suffrage to the existing possessors of the instruments of production." That is they would have, "the capitalist as ruler" whilst Socialists would vest all capitalist enterprise in the people's state. "The world is not to be regenerated by the old dogma of the Economists masquerading in Socialist dress", as the same writer says, speaking of Co-operation, in his lecture on "The Social Future of the Working-Classes". What is wanted is a power which shall moralize alike capital and labour, making their joint efforts a blessing to themselves and the world at large. "Therefore we must look for improvement not to this or that new-fangled industrial system, but to the creation of a moral and religious influence which may bend all to obedience to duty." Accordingly, he expresses his belief that "an organized religious influence will hereafter induce employers to concede to their men, voluntarily, a larger share of their profits than any Trades-Union could extort from them", though all along he argues in favour of Trades-Unionism as compared with Co-operation. His hope is in the concentration of capital in the hands of a "few chieftains of industry" organizing the workers, whose humble function will be invested with as much dignity as that of any other citizen who is doing his duty to society. Both will be influenced by "religion systematically promoted by an organized body of teachers". But, as Professor Beesly said in his paper read before the Conference for the Remuneration of Labour, "until public opinion has learned to regard the wealth of the Capitalist as a fund entrusted to him by society, to be administered for the benefit of society, and more especially of that particular group of workers for which he is responsible, no real and effectual improvement will take place in their condition". And again—"Religion will afford the principal systematic means of influencing the holders of wealth". This to him is the root of the matter. In short, all Comtists alike teach that the only remedy is the extinction of the "Old Adam of industrial selfishness" as Mr. Harrison calls it; "the solution of the industrial problem is a moral, social and religious question. Industry must be moralized." By means of moral education ours will cease to be a militant and become a pacific industry. The questions before us are, therefore: Has Positivism made sufficient progress thus far to encourage the hope of this moral as antecedent to the social regeneration becoming a fact? Who are its friends and its foes, and which will prevail? What headway has it made in the ranks of labour?

"We do not offer anything that can be called an alterative or specific to the socialist problem", says Mr. F. Harrison, in a private letter to the present writer in answer to some inquiries on this subject. "Agreeing with the Socialists on the fearful evils of the present industrial system, and also agreeing with them in repudiating the personal claims of this body, we insist that the entire social problem must be dealt with, we insist on an entire social reconstruction which must be based on Science and Religion teaching a new morality. Our answer to the problem put out by the Socialists is—the philosophical, religious, social scheme of Positivism." All then depends on the acceptableness of their system or the reverse if society is to be saved by Positivism as a social creed. Among the most favourable critics of Comte's system in this country figures first and foremost Professor Ingram, who, in his "History of Political Economy", speaks of the fourth volume of the *Philosophie Positive* as "a masterly exposition of sociological method", and who more or less adopts Comte's scientific theory of society. He, too, dwells emphatically on the revolution in the moral rather than the mechanical re-constitution of society, and so far from believing in the establishment of a co-operative commonwealth, such as Socialist writers foreshadow, he assumes with the Comtists the continued separation between the functions of the Capitalist and the Workman. He also with them looks forward to the time when both shall be regarded in the light of social functionaries. He, too, attaches great importance to the educational office of women in the family in raising the social tone of future generations of workmen, and he, too, expects from the growth of scientific culture and the triumph of sociological science that social improvement which results from the better regulation of functions in the society of the future. The curious fact has been pointed out by a foreign critic of Comte's system that whereas in France and Germany the system of Comte has been either rejected or neglected, in England it has met among many first-rate thinkers and economists with considerable attention and marked favour. Mill, Spencer, and others are mentioned as more or less influenced by Comtist ideas, and he assigns the following reasons. The ground here was prepared, he says, by the prevalence of realistic, as distinguished from idealistic, modes of thought, the Scientific as distinguished from the Utopian tendencies of English philosophers, and this more especially on account of the readiness of Comte's system to blend with Darwinism and the Evolution Theory, and because it coincided in point of time with the beginning of that current of economic speculation now in vogue which gives an historical and ethical interpretation of economic laws.* Whilst agreeing with this criticism, which is throughout fair and unimpassioned, we cannot help pointing out one or two additional reasons omitted why Positivism has found so much acceptance in this country. In the first place it is not unfriendly towards Individualism, *i.e.* Individualism modified by altruism, and in the next because it assigns an important function to Capitalism, nay it is desirous of creating a new chivalry of Industry as we have noticed already above; it is therefore not destruc-

* See "Auguste Comte und seine Bedeutung für die Entwickelung der Socialwissenschaft," von Dr. Heinrich Waentig, 1894, p. 211.

tive but constructive even on its most vulnerable side, its religion. For these reasons it commends itself to the common sense and better feelings of the English character. Among its friends in Germany, where its influence is felt less directly, Dr. Gerhart von Schulze Gävernitz must be reckoned. It is he who very aptly shows in his work on *Social Peace* in reference to this country that whatever difference may divide Socialists from Positivists, Socialism nevertheless is hailed by Positivism as helping in the propagation of its own theories for the following reasons: It emphasizes the duty of subordinating personal advantage to the common good; it compels the representatives of Individualism into giving due consideration to the social problem by inspiring them with a wholesome fear of a social revolt among the workers; it is a standing protest against the doctrine of *laissez faire* and the false idea of the unalterable natural laws of Political Economy which are supposed to defy any interference of human will; it paves the way to State interference where the welfare of the people is at stake: its impracticability will prevent it ever becoming a serious danger to society, so that whilst in the main promoting the diffusion of Comtist ideas as far as they affect society its powers of mischief have their natural limits.* Positivism, differs, however, as he points out, from Socialism in its defence of family life, in distinguishing state socialism from Socialism proper, in its demand for political decentralization, in favouring the development of Trades Unions, and in opposing all revolutionary methods as applied to social questions. And on the whole he considers Positivism

* "Zum socialen Frieden, eine Darstellung der socialpolitischen Erziehung des englischen Volkes im neunzehnten Jahrhundert," von Dr. Gerhart von Schulze Gävernitz, Vol. II. pp. 66 &c. and p. 72.

to have contributed largely towards that social peace which he considers is in a fair way of realization in this country.

In Germany the influence of Comtism has been less marked, and there ideas on Socialism most akin to Comte's system have been developed independently though contemporaneously, there are coincidences of thought between him and the precursors of sociological science, and the most recent representatives of social science in Germany who express general agreement with, though without drawing their inspiration from, Comte's system.

Among his adverse critics in this country the most formidable is Professor Caird, all the more so because he shews a large amount of sympathetic insight, and a complete freedom from theological bias. He points out that in his opposition to revolutionary individualism in such sayings as: "Man is a mere abstraction, and there is nothing real but Humanity"; Comte goes too far, though this is easily explained from the reaction which followed in Comte's time in the wake of those disappointments which the triumph of Positivism produced. He also with some of Comte's own followers characterises his religion in other respects as ineffectual both on account of its artificiality and the relativity of its worship, namely that of imperfect humanity, and because the cultus of space and the earth reintroduces theological fictions which Comte professes to destroy.

In the same way A. Toynbee shewed that to build on the materialistic basis, as Comte does, a system of altruistic religion and to hold up to humanity an abstraction as the "Supreme Being" for its object of devotion, is a feeble substitute for current creeds; whilst Mr. Kidd says of the religion of humanity that it is incapable, from the nature of its conditions, of exercising the functions of a religion in the evolution of Society.* But Caird's main contention is that "Comte so decidedly breaks with the democratic spirit of modern times, and seeks to set up an aristocracy in the State and a monarchy in the Church," and that it is the "patriciate", influenced indeed by the Proletariate, but still the Patriciate and not the populace which will have "to direct and regulate the industrial life of the community".†

This, it appears to us, is the weakest point in Comtism, both as a scheme for the solution of the social problem, and as a new philosophy for the working-classes. It brings us to the next, the crucial question: How far does it commend itself to the masses of the people, and what is the attitude of Socialists towards it as a social system?

We turn to France, where it is presumably best understood and where its chances of success have been better, to say the least of it, than in foreign countries, we turn to a number of the *Revue Socialiste* for April 1888 and there we find the opening article by H. Amiel occupied with Comte's *Philosophie Positive*. It serves as an introduction to a number of subsequent articles on the same subject. It speaks respectfully of *la grande découverte* of A. Comte, and in answer to the two questions to which the writer addresses himself, namely:—Is it possible to draw a *morale* or exact theory of rights and duties from the Positivist Philosophy? and, this being settled, is it able to create a common faith founded on scientific demon-

* "Social Evolution", p. 115 by Kidd.
† See "The Social Philosophy and Religion of Comte" by Edward Caird, 1893, pp. 200—202.

stration, a faith as strong and cohesive as that which formerly subjected man under the yoke of theological dogma,—he gives an affirmative reply to the former. As to the latter he speaks doubtfully. Comtism has not been able to rally all minds around its standard. At the same time he deprecates the non-success of a system which might heal all existing intellectual dissensions, more especially since its chief merit consists in finding a way of reconciling the two great tendencies of the day, the one making for order, the other for progress. Moreover, he shews that what should chiefly recommend Comtism to Socialists is the three salient doctrines that property, like work from which it takes its rise is, "social in its source and social in its destiny"; that society is not a collection of individuals engaged in mutual struggles, but that all men, on the contrary, are "*travailleurs solidaires moralement égaux*"; and that all our social functions are "*des agents de la collectivité*". Here we see much sympathy on the part of Socialism with Comtism.* But in a later number of the same Review (December 1891) referring to a lecture given by a member of the "*Cercle des Proletaires Positivistes*" on the current economic theories of contemporary Socialism, delivered before a mixed audience containing Collectivists and Communists, we are distinctly told that it was no easy task for the lecturer to obtain a fair hearing in spite of the multifarious points of contact between Positivism and Collectivism in their critique of *Bourgeois Egoisme*. Cultured

* In a recent article of the *Revue Socialiste* by Dr. Délon on "La Vie Sociale, la Morale et le Progrès", he says "*le mouvement socialiste contemporain doit être considéré comme l'éveil du sens social et comme la manifestation du besoin d'une solidarisation plus complète.*" This, too, is the chief object of Positivism.

Socialists, no doubt, can see many points of contact between their own theories and those of Comte, but even they are in direct antagonism to its religious cult, whilst the rank and file of Socialists are naturally repelled from a system which offers so little by way of immediate and tangible benefits for their class, and only promises in the far future what it calls ambiguously the ultimate incorporation of the workers with the general scheme of Society. The materialistic conceptions of Socialists as a body, and their implicit faith in mechanical rearrangements of Society, are opposed to the spiritual views and belief in moral dynamics of Comtism. Thus its scientific treatment of the Social problem puts an intellectual strain on those who would become its disciples; and its sublime ethical standard is too much even for the most ideal of French workmen. The prospect of a future point in time when "each man's moral faculty shall be such as leads him to control all those desires which run counter to the good of mankind," to use Professor Huxley's happy phrase, has no attraction for the untutored intellect of man in the mass. Yet it is this on which the whole system of Comtist Sociology moves as on a pivot. Comte in 1848 thought it would require a generation for the "previous reconstruction of opinions and habits of life upon the basis laid down by Positivism" in order to bring about a Social revolution. A generation and a half has passed away and Socialism has overtaken Positivism as the ruling social creed of the masses in France and the rest of Europe. The reason is not far to seek. It promises palpable and immediate advantages to the labourer, it powerfully appeals to the passions, and does not make any large demands on intellectual and moral effort. "Socialism," as one of its representatives said in the cultured organ of the party in England ten years ago, "nobly attempts, not, like Positivism, to educate the good and to convert the wicked, but to establish such an arrangement of the social relations of mankind so as to prevent at the outset the tragical catastrophes which cause the pain and the misery of this life. *

Dr. Congreve, in answer to a letter of enquiry by the present writer as to the steps taken by Comtists to win over the workmen on whom Comte himself so confidently rests for support in the spread of his system, replies, "There are two ways in which practical work is done: (1) by the formation of a right Social feeling from which will come a strong impulse towards meeting the social wants; (2) organizing some new or aiding some older movement with that end in view. The first method we steadily pursue. For the second we are hardly as yet in a condition to attempt it. We must become more numerous and more endowed with material means. In short, for the present there is no organized Social work." The Positivist Society with which Mr. F. Harrison is connected has its lectures and addresses, its classes, its Young Men's and Women's Guild in connection with Newton Hall, Fetter Lane. Judging from the reports of them kindly sent to us by Mr. Harrison, the aim and object of English Positivists is the spread of general culture, moral as well as intellectual, among their adherents rather than active propagation among outsiders. Comtism trusts to the spread of its ideas with the widening of the intellect

* *To-day*, Volume 2, No. 11, p. 467, and see article also No. 9 of the same Volume two articles on "Pessimism, Positivism and Socialism" by Franz Ludwig Lehmann.

of European nations generally. It is Evolutionary,* not Revolutionary, and for this very reason is not likely to make headway among Socialists whose watchword is the Social Revolution.

"Le rapport du groupe des Prolétaires Positivistes est "opposé au principe de la lutte des classes; il ne croit "pas à l'efficacité de la révolution violente; le rapport est "une véritable dissertation de ce groupe en faveur de "l'évolution pacifique. L'assemblée se montre défavorable "aux conclusions de ce rapport."

Such was the judgment passed on the report of the Positivist workmen at the eighth Annual Congress of the "*Union Fédérative du Centre*" of the most moderate Socialist party in Paris a few years ago. It is matched by the expression of opinion of three Positivist workmen delegates at *Congrès Ouvrier* in 1877, in three discourses on technical education, the representation of the Proletariat in Parliament and co-operative societies. What they recommend respectively is general education in encyclopædic

* Comte agrees with K. Marx that Social Evolution is a necessary process fixed by the condition of things, that all follows in the course of natural development and that therefore all social action is bounded by the limits of the social milieu or environment. But whereas Marx believes that the final goal is a social revolution to dethrone capital, Comte looks forward to the reign of altruistic principles in an industrial world where the Capitalist is Commander-in-chief. All we can do according to Comte is to remove impediments in the way of natural evolution; to assist the birth of the new age is our duty according to K. Marx. "Organize knowledge and cultivate the affections and social harmony will follow" says Comte. "Organise yourselves," says Marx to the labourers, "and dethrone Capitalism by your united strength, and you will reign for ever and ever."

† See "Le Positivisme au Congrès ouvrier: Discours des Citoyens Laporte, Magnin et Finance", p. 6 et passim.

knowledge for both sexes, in addition to technical training, so as to have not only the power to vote but the power of voting rightly, and also education on the plan of co-operative trades unions supported by public opinion, and they recommend increased production and a more equalized distribution of wealth, *i.e.* social reforms consequent on moral and mental improvement, but no violent change in the status quo. The fact is that Positivism does not appeal to the impatient cupidity of the masses, claiming a larger share in the good things of this world, but it preaches self-abnegation, devotion to the common good, suppression of the selfish feelings and a merging of self-love in universal philanthropy. It disavows all attempts to destroy, it only believes in building on the old foundation according to circumstances, favouring this or that moderate measure of reform suitable to the times. For this reason it preaches to empty benches. Even the cultured few remain deaf to its exhortations and are scarcely moved by its touching appeals to worship and to serve the human race. Not only the man of common clay, who cares little for humanity but much for himself, is apt to say in the words put into his mouth by Mr. Mallock:* "You must promise something to each of us or very certainly you will be able to promise nothing to all of us"; but even the higher class of mind, when called upon to love and cherish Humanity as his own flesh, knowing what average Humanity is, will be tempted to say with Edmund Scherer: "As for myself the human species amuses me and interests me, but in its totality it inspires me neither with veneration nor tenderness; I

---

* "Is Life Worth Living", pp. 52, etc.

decline solidarity".* But if neither *les philosophes* nor the populace will accept the Positivist system for their guiding principle in social life what is to become of it as the social creed of the age? From the leaders of thought and from the manual toilers Comte expected in the first instance the acceptance of his system. Hitherto the latter have shown no great willingness to accept it. It has given stimulus, and does so still, to scientific enquiry and to the ethical fervour of fine minds whom the popular religion no longer inspires with enthusiasm, but as a scheme of social reconstruction it has thus far proved a failure.

* *Fortnightly Review*, April 1889, p. 596.

CHAPTER VI.

SOCIALISM AND CULTURE.

> "The change through which they passed was..... the rise of the race to a new phase of existence with an illimitable vista of progress, their minds were affected in all their faculties with a stimulus of which the outburst of the mediæval renaissance offers a suggestion but a faint one indeed; there ensued an era of mechanical invention, scientific discovery, art, music, and literary productiveness to which no previous age of the world offers anything comparable."
>
> "*Looking Backward.*"

"CULTURE and Socialism are transmuting everything," wrote the late Mr. F. Adams in the *Fortnightly Review* of December 1893, *i.e.* next to the importance attached to the social problems of the day, comes culture in its claims on the modern man. In Socialism labour vents its grievances and gives expression to its hopes. Among the leisured classes culture, or the demand for a wider diffusion of the luxuries of the mind, takes the first place among the desiderata of the hour. The questions before us are these, How far do the two movements react on each other? Are they compatible?

"I write every line I write," said Lassalle, the leader

of German Social-Democracy, to his opponent, "armed with the whole culture of my century". But this was not the intellectual condition of the great body of his followers. True, in the preamble of the Gotha programme, now superseded by that of Erfurt from which the phrase is omitted, we are told that "Labour is the source of all wealth and all *culture*". But this only means that the "cultured few" are what they are through the unpaid and appropriated work of the untutored many; the means of culture are claimed as a right, they are not here considered as a possession.

On the other hand the professors of the religion of culture, such as David Strauss, the well-known exponent of the new faith as against the old, express their undisguised fear of the ultimate triumph of the ignorant multitude led by socialistic agitators. They speak of them as "the Huns and Vandals of our modern Culture, more dangerous than the former since they come not from a distance, but live in our midst". In the same way the pessimist von Hartmann, pointing to the undoubted historical fact that culture has always been the possession of a minority, expects nothing but evil from the establishment of the social-democratic state and a corruption among its chief office holders which will open the door to an amount of coarseness, meanness, and immorality greater than that prevailing under the official corruption in Russia, Turkey or the United States taken together. Others, eminent in different departments of literature might be quoted, entertaining similar ideas as to the antagonism which it is asserted exists between socialism and culture, as, indeed, there are not wanting socialists who speak with as much contempt of culture as there are cultured persons without number who feel instinctively that the luxury of leisured learning is incompatible with socialistic principles.

It will be interesting, then, to note in the first place the relation of the cultured classes towards socialism and then that of socialism towards culture.

"Culture," said the late Principal Shairp in his little book on *Culture and Religion,* "is a literary and æsthetic product", and as such is wanting in that "brotherly impulse" which shall "touch the universal ground on which men are one". This, we may add, finds its illustration in the contemptuous manner in which the great poets like Shakespeare and Goethe treat social and socialistic claims. Even Tennyson, though never contemptuous, is exceedingly cautious, and in his later utterances is cold if not scornful when he touches on social problems and their solution.

On the other hand, it is an indisputable fact that among the working-classes in towns the cultivation of literature in all its branches and the study of natural science in particular have been developed to a considerable extent. The reviews and lesser prints circulating among continental socialists, and the books in their collections reprinted and sold at a low price, are such as to tax the highest intellectual powers and such as are certainly far above the ken of those middle-class critics of socialism who talk so glibly of the ignorance of the masses, their own ignorance and inability to enjoy the delight of true culture being as great if not greater than that of the objects of their professed commiseration and contempt.

What the socialist objects to is not culture in itself, but culture as a luxury enjoyed by the rich only. "Much of our so-called "culture" is based on a hideous superstructure of degradation and suffering," complains Mr. H. S. Salt, one of the most cultured of socialists, in the January number of the *New Review* for 1891, where he defends his socialist followers against the charge of indifference to and enmity towards Culture as such. And in this we find Principal Shairp agreeing with him. He, too, objects to "theories of self-culture which exalt man's natural self-seeking into a specious and refined philosophy of life". He, too, shows, though in a different manner, that in order to become a "beneficent power", culture must not be enjoyed in "selfish isolation and self-complacent seclusion from the common crowd of illiterates".

From this it would appear that the assumed antagonism between socialism and culture is not proven. But let us examine a little more minutely the Socialist's account of the matter as far as literature and art are concerned and then see what his individualist opponent has to say in reply.

Mr. Salt, in the article referred to, speaks of the probable effects of socialism on literature and "the coming nationalization of letters". He points out that in a state where riches and poverty are unknown, where private simplicity and public munificence go hand in hand, there is no room for the literary dilettante or the literary drudge; no one would write either for amusement or ambition, still less from avaricious motives, but only from a deep sense of responsibility in fulfilment of duty. From this revolution in the literary profession he expects the best results; only good books would be published, no more *éditions de luxe* to gratify pride of possession among the idle rich, no more Grub-street purveyors of books that will sell to keep the penniless authors alive on the brink of starvation. For in the socialist community, where all work and where labour hours are reduced to a minimum; accordingly there will be more leisure for all and with it a large influx of appreciative readers. And, in a state of society where all are provided for and no anxieties for maintenance in material comforts exist, there will be no writers who write for bread. Therefore, "if the literature of the future is to be something more than a sickly hot-house exotic, it must draw its sustenance from the subsoil of a just and humanly organized community—which is socialism". The money spent by the state now in armaments will then be spent in libraries and other national treasuries of knowledge accessible to all alike. The literary class as such will disappear with every form of class *régime,* and the literary ideal will be raised with the growing sense of brotherhood and equality. Brotherly rivalry to produce the best for the common good will take the place of competition for the highest place in the literary Olympus and the largest fortunes made in the literary market. The whole people, and not the plutocracy, will be the literary patrons, or rather patronage will be out of date; all will be lovers of literature and literature will be an occupation to which authors turn for the love of it and of those they desire to benefit, which is the whole community.

Therefore "the true lover of literature has nothing to fear, but, on the contrary, everything to hope, from socialism". There is only one class of literary men who will find no encouragement in occupation then, and that is the critic, because we suppose they are what Disraeli said of them, the men who have fallen short of literary success. For in a perfect state of society there will be no failures whatever. There the socialist writer becomes a law unto himself, independent of the laws of style, and treatment, and the approved canons of criticism. Literature, no longer a combination, as now, of truth and trifling, becomes a serious business which spurns to provide a pabulum for the "literary mob". In fact, this body has ceased to exist and with it the critic's calling to select and comment on the "best books" of the season.

The *Belles-lettres* of socialism will require no selection, they will all be select as they are all excellent.

We have not noticed in the perusal of socialist literature, either in prose or verse, anything to cause anxiety to literary critics on this head. Their extinction for want of opportunity of exercising their function has not yet become a matter of urgency. Our socialist literati, living as they do in an individualist society and still influenced by its ways, will naturally for a little while continue to share its shortcomings. Further on—well, *nous verrons!* At present we cannot say in applying the Psalmist's words to socialist writings, "I have seen an end of all perfection".

Matthew Arnold, in his book on "Culture and Anarchy", shows that the democratic force which is aiming to supersede the middle-class liberalism is in no better frame of mind in relation to culture than its deadly foe, that it has little of *that inward spiritual activity, having for its characters increased sweetness, increased light, increased life, increased sympathy,* which he considers to be the outcome of true culture. It has fire and force, but it lacks lucidity and spirituality. The materialistic individualism of the revolution clings to the leading spirits of the social revolution, nay, the extreme socialists, the professors of the Nihilistic Creed, as described by Tourgenieff in his novels, drawn from life, display a considerable rancour against every species of culture, while extolling the study of natural science, and this simply because applied science tends to the material comfort of the people. "I prefer a piece of cheese to the whole of Pushkin," wrote the nihilist poet Nekrassow. So, too, Tzchernyschewki in his nihilist novel abstains from every form of æsthetic embellishment and eschews all forms of literary refinement so that he may adhere strictly to fact.

Socialists may reject this testimony as coming from the extreme wing of their party from whom in many respects they differ. But we have read an article superscribed "*Cant and Culture*" in *Justice,* the true tenor of which goes far to prove that the love of culture and the tone of mind which is required for a due appreciation of poetry and art generally are wanting in the out-and-out social-democrat. He is too much absorbed in the material demands he makes on society, and too agitated in the virulence of his class-hatred, to enjoy that calm collectedness and liberation of mind which attunes it for æsthetic contemplation. The "ways of Jacobinism", as Mr. Arnold calls them, are not the paths of pleasantness by which travel the devotees of literature and art.

On the other hand, though in a sense it is true, as Mr. Arnold says, that "the men of culture are the apostles of equality", because ideal goods in literature and art are or may be the common property of all. Yet the cleavage between the aristocracy of talent and democratic levellers-down does exist, and the sympathy of the cultured classes is not with the uncultured masses in most of their aspirations. "The most cultured are the least social," says Dr. Congreve, and we may add only socialistic in a patronizing way, which the masses resent. When culture shall have accomplished its work of harmoniously perfecting Humanity in all directions and developing all its powers this gulf no doubt will be bridged over. But it is culture as the study of moral and spiritual perfection which must accomplish this.

In the mean time we find even such cultured socialists as Mr. E. Belfort Bax averring that the intellectual and moral revolution of society rests primarily upon the conditions in which its wealth is produced and distributed. This is exactly that belief in machinery and system which Mr. Arnold regards as the bane of culture. "Culture looks beyond machinery," he says, and we fully agree with him, "culture hates hatred; culture has one great passion, the passion for sweetness and light.... it knows that the sweetness and light of the few must be imperfect until the raw and unkindled masses of humanity are touched with sweetness and light." Here we see the apostles of culture and the apostles of the new social gospel as wide apart as they possibly could be in a matter of principle. The latter require a material and mechanical basis for social reconstruction whereas the former would build on a mental and moral foundation.

"The growth of any real art, culture, or sentiment, in the slimy ooze of greed and profitmongering" is impossible, says Mr. Belfort Bax. "The sterner self of populace likes bawling, hustling, and smashing the lighter self, and beer," says Mr. Arnold contemptuously of the social agitator and his followers.

There is a vast amount of truth in both. True culture, not the spurious culture which Mr. Bax attacks, will produce the frame of mind required in all classes which will improve ultimately the framework of society. Culture as such is the enemy of social anarchy. But the means of culture and the power of that "free play of thought", which Mr. Arnold so much desiderates, amid the rush of philistinistic getting-on and the turmoil of popular agitation, this free play of thought is impossible to men at the grindstone of daily want, working for mere subsistence wages, engaged in the struggle for existence, and living from hand to mouth. Therefore some social reforms and methods of redistribution of the ordinary wants of Humanity will have to be adopted which will render intellectual and ethical culture possible and accessible to the largest number.

There is one test, and it is an infallible test, by which we may discover how far some form of socialism, introduced in the course of social reforms or otherwise may eventually prove the true friend or enemy of culture, and that is the work done already in literature and art by socialists coping with their individualist rivals; socialism has already produced its works of fiction, its poetry. It has made attempts in art criticism, not to speak of its *pièces de resistance* in books treating on political economy, and essay writing, as *e.g.* in the Fabian Essays and the rest. A short examination of a few specimens of socialist *Belles-Lettres* may help us, therefore, in determining to some extent what are its claims as the promoter of culture.

We will take the socialist novel to begin with, for here the literary success of socialists has been most conspicuous.

By socialist novels * we mean fictions by socialists or their sympathizers, depicting the society of the future from their own stand-point. In them, as a matter of course, the present social order serves only as a foil to throw into

* For a fuller treatment of this subject see an article by the present writer in Lippincott's *Monthly Magazine* for January 1895.

distinct view the glowing colours and enticing brilliancy of this ideal scheme. We have not here the picture of man conquering the lions as in the fable, but the lions painting their own picture in a leonine rage against all that is, to show what might be. The socialist novel thus becomes a work of historical imagination, but historical in the future-perfect tense, as in "Looking Backward", where a bold attempt is made to describe retrospectively the course of social transformation finally effected in the year 2000 of our era. It is the case of Macaulay's New Zealander reversed. Instead of this son of the New World sitting on an arch of London Bridge and meditating on the fallen greatness of England, we have a New England man waking out of a century's sleep in the American Athens and rubbing his eyes in wonder at the mighty social changes brought about during that lapse of time.

This affords an excellent opportunity for interesting comparison and contrast between the old order and the new. The socialist fiction, like so many novels of the period, becomes thus a convenient vehicle for moralizing and philosophizing reflection.

The most notable examples are Tchernichewsky's "What is to be done?" and Bellamy's "Looking Backward", both stories which have appeared in two young countries with a future before them,—Russia and America,—resembling one another in this particular, that their social institutions were introduced from Western Europe and planted on virgin soil, that in both these countries the gradations peculiar to the old societies are wanting, but with this difference, that in one of these countries political freedom exists in all its plenitude, while in the other the reverse is the case,—a most important difference, affecting the growth of social institutions and the methods of giving effect to aspirations after social improvement. Thus, the title of the Russian novel, "What is to be done?" at once suggests the hopelessly confused state of the Russian mind brought face to face with this modern problem, almost a state of mind bordering on despair, while "Looking Backward" expresses the hopeful outlook into the future as the characteristic trait of the giant Republic, with its big strides of progress, taking a century by a single step.

But for picturesque aspects of Russian socialism and a true picture of the life of the people we must look to such novels as Tourgenieff's "Fathers and Sons", or "Virgin Soil" and "Smoke", and to Gogol's affecting pictures of misery and hopelessness among the masses, as in that remarkable story, "Dead Souls", in which the leading character is a dealer in dead serfs who are still counted as living and attached to this or that piece of land and mortgaged at the bank, a real "traffic in human souls" of the most ghastly nature.

In the English romance "A More Excellent Way", we find the socialist novel in its infancy. Judging by the opinions expressed by socialists themselves, this tale expresses fully their views and aspirations.

It is taken up principally with arguments to show the exceeding evil of that "trinity of evil, rent, profit, and interest". This exposes it to the same criticism which we had to apply to the Russian novel, though perhaps in a less degree, for we have here neither the venomous bitterness against the existing social order peculiar to the Russian story, nor the extravagant expectation entertained of social changes in the future, as in Mr. Bellamy's story, but simply strictures and occasional good-humoured hits at narrow prejudices, compromising respectabilities, and commonplace limitations in the social life of the upper middle class, or at the worst, severe diatribes directed against the falsities and fatuous imbecilities of ordinary English life, ending with a damnatory sentence such as this: "Yes, our civilization is a sham."

Comparing the stories written by others about socialism, such as Gissing's "Demos", or Grant Allen's "Philistia", or Sime's "King Capital", or even Mallock's anti-socialist novel, "The Old Order Changeth", we are again bound to state that the presentment of the movement as given by the onlooker is superior both in interest and insight to that of those actually inside it, possibly because calm consideration of social facts and a judicial frame of mind in calculating social and anti-social forces cannot be expected from those who are engaged in the conflict, while a collected manner in dealing with the facts as the foundation of socialist fiction is essential to produce a perfect picture for the general reader.

This power of dispassionate reflection we should *a priori* expect to find in the German socialist novel, self-recollectedness, even where the fervour of the social passion is strongest, being a characteristic of this nation of thinkers. Moreover, the consciousness of strength which socialists possess in a high degree in the country where in numbers, intelligence, and perfect organization socialism has advanced all along the line, should lead us to expect that ease and elasticity of mind which enable the writer to attend to literary finish. In order to do this we want a tolerant gentleness in dealing with human infirmities and a tender regard for social prejudices, with the power of seeing the poetic side of even faulty social institutions whilst emphasizing the necessity of social reforms. And this we actually meet with in the socialist novel of Germany in "Kranke Herzen",—"Sick Hearts",—by Otto Walster, the recognized socialist novelist. Here we have two novelettes, with clever plots, excellent drawings of natural scenery, and a sentimental interpretation of nature, by one who is far from being unacquainted with the mysteries of natural science.

In traversing the field of literature of this kind in diverse countries, we find that where socialism is weakest, as in Russia, it assumes the character of the "literature of revolt", because galled into a tone of desperation by official persecution; that where it still haunts the mind of the cultured few, as in the days when Emerson and Hawthorne made Brook Farm a social Utopia, there its hopefulness is very pronounced, extravagant expectations finding their encouragement in the efflorescence of natural progress and prosperity; that where full liberty of speech and action is granted, as in England, the socialist literature in the form of the novel becomes most harmless; that it appears in its best form, as to manner and matter, in the country where socialism has become most perfectly organized, and where this kind of prose-poetry fitly expresses the social ideal in a tone of elevation and a freedom from passionate excitement which augurs well for the future of literature should socialism be permitted to celebrate the triumphs it vaunts. From our survey it would appear that the fears entertained by some leading men of culture, lest socialism should be making havoc of all literature, are rather exaggerated and unreasonable.

In France alone, where socialism, like society, has become most prosaic, no novels of this kind—except perhaps "Jacques Vingtras" by Jules Vallès—have been produced of late years. In the "*Cri du Peuple*", a daily paper much read by socialists and at one time rendered popular by the novels of Vallès (which, however, were not socialistic novels), M. Zola and his school furnish the *feuilleton*; and realistic novels are largely advertised by the principal socialist bookseller of Paris as presumably the pabulum most acceptable to the socialist novel-readers of France. From which it would appear that as the centre of gravity of socialism, as an intellectual ideal, has moved from France to Germany, so the absence of the socialist novel in France marks the decadence of socialism itself, and indicates a descent from a higher and more spiritual to a lower and more material conception of its claims. It represents the most recent form of French socialism, with its lacklustre practicalities, commonplace aims, and bald demands for increased opportunities of self-indulgence.

Thus it would seem that the extinction of the socialist novel implies a degradation of socialism itself, and that its further development in artistic perfection will depend on the higher mental and moral elevation of socialism regarded in the light of a social aspiration, a principle which it is well to bear in mind at a time when the novel occupies so important a place in literature.

This leads to the further consideration of the attitude of socialism towards scientific culture. Here socialism is on firmer ground. It professes to be, and in a certain sense is, scientific. It is above all things leaning on natural science, and that alone, for support in its theories and demands, for the latter are mainly as we have pointed out, for the present at least, of a material nature. And accordingly we find a number of scientific works especially by writers of the materialistic school of thought included in the Library of Literature advertised in the socialist press. But here, again, we observe that the aim and object of the socialist in his pursuit of scientific culture is not of the broader and deeper sort which cultivates science for the sake of obtaining large views of the universe, but for the sole purpose apparently of entering better equipped into the arena of class struggles armed with scientific knowledge to make war against religion and the social institutions founded on it, so that in the conflict between science and religion socialism may help in demolishing the foundation of society laid in pre-scientific times. "The ideality of the scientific sense" is wanting. The forces of Nature are to be studied to make them serviceable to man's material comfort and only indirectly to the enlargement of his mental range, and the victories of physical science are regarded simply as the prelude to the victory of the Proletariat over the forces of nature and modern civilization.

From all this it will be seen that the instinctive fears of the literary class, lest the progress of science, art, learning, and the general development of man's capacities might suffer in the event of socialism carrying the day, are not altogether ill-founded. On the other hand we see that the instinct of the socialist is correct which prompts him to demand that all the treasures of knowledge and culture in science, art, and literature should become a common possession. He is jealous even in Germany of intellectual superiority in his leaders, the individual "*Capacitäten*", because these are determined to rule the roost. He will not tolerate even an aristocracy of talent.

Here, then, we have the historic war between aristocracy

and democracy in a new form. It finds its reconciliation in a levelling-up process which is equally opposed to the fallacy of exclusiveness in the cultured few who affect a dread of the "coming slavery" of socialism, and is also opposed to the fallacy of levelling down by depression of the eminent so as to bring about equality on the part of the Proletariat for fear of the "modern slavery" of Capital. The latter is like an attempt to rase mountains and hills to the even ground so as to make all a plane on the sea level, though the billows of the sea rise mountain high, thus violating the sacred principle of natural equality.

When the modern socialist shall have been taught, after getting over the worst of his sordid cares and narrowing anxieties of life, that man does not live by bread alone, and when labour more efficiently organized, as in some state-departments like the post-office, shall have a more ample share of cultured leisure; when the principle of educating the mind whilst administering liberally to the wants of the body, adopted by the co-operative central board, shall, with the farther spread of co-operation, be used as a means of spreading general culture combined with a careful study of social science both in its ideal and practical aspects; when mechanics' institutions and socialist clubs shall make it their principal aim not only to raise the mental calibre of their members with a view to class-organization, but to make the ideal goods of man available for all as the prime source of inner enlightenment and joy; when the tentative efforts to create a popular stage such as Schiller and other great patriots and friends of popular culture have at all times longed to call into existence, shall render it once more the great educating power of the people, as it was in Greece; when the culture of religion, not excluded from the rest of the means of culture, shall have become a powerful instrument for the development of man's spiritual nature—then the possibility of realizing the social ideal which has haunted the human mind since the very earliest formation of society may be brought within reasonable distance. An ideal commonwealth thus rises before us in which all the wealth of art, of science and literature shall be the common property of all. This would preclude the danger of the few belonging to the idle classes becoming enervated by the enjoyment of an overluxurious civilization, for each citizen would be kept in perfect health of body and mind by a wise alternation of labour and refreshment, activity and contemplation, whilst the even-paced pursuit of the ideal and the practical in due proportion among all would finally bring about that harmonious development of all the faculties which is aimed at in the methods, and expected from the spread, of higher culture.

CHAPTER VII.

ART AND ANARCHY

> "We inscribe in letters of gold over the portal of Art, the command to eat, drink, and be merry, for to-morrow we die, carefully explaining, it is true, that this is to be interpreted in the most refined and catholic sense.... Goethe is our great and patron saint. All the artists, poets, painters, musicians and writers believe in the hunt for happiness."
>
> F. ADAMS.

> "The aim of art is to increase the happiness of men, by giving them beauty and interest of incident to amuse their leisure, and prevent them wearying even of rest, and by giving them hope and bodily pleasure in their work; or, shortly, to make man's work happy and his rest fruitful."
>
> W. MORRIS.

ON the subject of art culture we have every reason to listen respectfully to Mr. W. Morris, the poet, artist, and socialist; nor could we select a more competent spokesman or a more worthy representative.

What then has art to do with anarchy, or socialism with æsthetics, according to this authority, a man of the most cultivated taste in poetry, one well acquainted with the technicalities of art; what has such a one to say on the relationship between Art and Socialism ? Writing in the number of the *New Review* already quoted, on the socialist ideal of art, he tells us that socialism as an all-embracing theory of life has its own æsthetic as well as its ethic and religion, that inequality of condition has now become incompatible with the existence of healthy art, and that art must become again the common possession of the whole people if it is to live and flourish as in the Middle Ages, when all handicraft aimed at the production of that which is beautiful. Carrying the war into the enemy's camp Mr. Morris declares that our present commercial civilization actually is hostile to art and possesses none of those finer perceptions which the love of art implies because of its "utilitarian brutality". The socialist "instead of looking upon art as a luxury incidental to a certain privileged position" claims it "as a necessity of human life which society has no right to withhold from anyone of the citizens." In the socialist state, therefore, all work would cease to be drudgery, pleasure would accompany the labour of production, and with Ruskin his master Morris would say that "all human work depends for its beauty on the happy life of the workman", that the joyous performance of the labour renders it "a thing of beauty which is a joy for ever".

Art, therefore, must not be kept alive as now by a small group of artists depending on wealthy but mostly vulgar purchasers. To be effective on a large scale, as a power forwarding all life, it must become the object of harmonious co-operation among neighbours, as in the craft-gilds of the Middle Ages; it must cease to be the art of a clique and become the art of the whole people, since "the pleasurable exercise of our energies is at once the source of all art and the cause of all happiness: that is to say the end of life".

In his "Letters from Nowhere" he amply illustrates this theory, and gives a picture of its practical working a century after this "new birth of art in modern times" has been brought about by the social revolution. In a lecture on Art and Socialism delivered before the Secular Society of Leicester in 1884, in which he severely criticizes the hideousness of the rich man's palace of art and shows the impossibility of true art culture in an age given up to the pursuit of material prosperity, he says broadly:

"The beginnings of the social revolution must be the foundations of the rebuilding of the art of the people, that is to say of the pleasure of life."

Replying to this in a subsequent paper in the *New Review* on the individualist side, Mr. Mallock has no difficulty in showing that there was more inequality in the Venice of Titian than in the London of Millais, that the division of classes in Florence, when art flourished most in that city of merchant princes, was greater than in Liverpool or Manchester of the present day, that society in Athens was based on slavery, that labour is ceasing to be artistic now not because of the inequality of fortunes but on account of the minute division of labour which does not permit any given worker to produce any one piece of work as a whole. He quotes Mr. Whistler as his authority for saying that the real reason why the mediæval artisan was more of an artist was because he had more time to bestow on his work, that wares then were more artistic than they are now because there were fewer wares turned out, and what there was was done with more love for the work because there was more leisure.

The latter is a fatal admission on the part of the individualist, for it is the reduction of labour hours with the wider diffusion of labour that socialists demand for the very purpose of extending culture. There is more truth in the correction of history. No doubt, at all times the labour of the many has been conducive to the cultivation of art and literature among the few, so that even Buckle derives from this a specious argument in favour of slavery as the pre-requisite of early civilization. But the main question here is whether the tone and tenor, whether the temperament of the modern mechanic or machine labourer, is such that, if socialism gained the victory, art would find in him a true patron and he again in his work would become a true artist; so that "art made by the people for the people" would become as Mr. Morris tells us in his lectures on the Hopes and Fears of Art, "a joy to the maker and the user". This is the real point at issue between the modern socialist and his opponent. Comte imagined, too, that, with the establishment of the new social doctrine he taught, a wide field would be opened to the cultivation of the arts, and that it was only necessary "to exhort the working-classes to seek happiness in calling their moral and mental powers into constant exercise, and to give them an education, the principal basis of which is æsthetic", in order "to place art under the protection of its natural patrons". But a real knowledge of the workman as he is, as distinguished from the imaginary type as he is pictured in the brain of the philosopher and the socialist prophet, renders it very doubtful whether this is a well-founded hope.

In the meantime, as T. Labusquière said at the inauguration of the monument erected to André Gill the artist in 1887, whilst defending his friends against the charge of being radicals and '*anti-artistes*': "The labourers, the revolutionary party, want to bring about the *material emancipation* of humanity so as to make sure of their moral and intellectual emancipation." But is it not the moral and spiritual change which as such must precede the formation of a superior system of society? In the course of this natural development we shall reap the riper fruits of a heightened civilization which make the cultivation of literature and art on a larger scale possible and efficacious, and make man more indifferent to material enjoyments.

Here again by their fruits ye shall know them. What have socialists done in the art of poetry? As to the poems produced by modern socialism, it has been remarked by those apparently not too well acquainted with the subject, that they form a complete failure, that they are wanting (at least in this country) in vigour and earnest passion and bear no comparison with the Chartist poems of a past generation. Those who prefer this objection attribute the fault to the unreality of the socialist creed itself; feeling and inspiration are wanting, they say, in socialist poems, because the movement is lacking actuality.

But this is not true altogether of English productions and still less so of continental poetry of the kind. As we shall presently show, from a few examples given, the poetry of socialism in form and substance does not reach a very high level, nor does it fulfil the highest function of the art as "expressing in beautiful form and melodious language the best thoughts and the subtlest feelings which the spectacle of life awakens in the finest souls". It resembles modern poetry generally in being critical, not creative; it is not the poetry of reflection, but rather that of passion, rarely rising to the dignity of meditative stateliness in dwelling on the darker aspects and deeper significance of social life. It is, and pretends to be nothing else but, "*une poésie lyrique de l'opposition*". It has a flavour of Byronic scorn, and is tinged with the bitterness of gall as are some of the poems of Heine, but it lacks the ferocious force of the former and the fine though mordant irony of the latter.

Take, *e.g.* the following concluding stanza of a poem by Joynes, the former Eton master, chosen from his "Socialist Rhymes". Its object is to show the fallacy of natural inequality:

> Away we'll dash the tyrant's lash,
> So rouse yourselves, my hearties,
> To slay and slash, to smite and smash
> Their cursed game of parties.
> Our hearts, God wot, may well wax hot,
> To think how we've been cheated—
> 'Twill be our lot with steel and shot
> To see our foes defeated.

This sort of thing is sheer rubbish.

Mr. H. S. Salt's poems, published under the collective title "Rhyme and Reason", contain many happy *aperçus*, or choice bits of sarcastic banter, which rarely reach, however, the high level of the real poetry of satire. They show a certain amount of dexterous handling, however, and are pungent, brisk, and often humorous. "Hodge's Dream" and "A Song of Freedom" read smoothly as *vers de société*, and others there are which swell into trenchant declamation. But though all contain some sharp, barbed arrows well directed against some forms of faithless religion and heartless philanthropy, as in "The Blessings of Content" and the "Hymn to Malthus", they are wanting in the power of artistic touch and fine discrimination; there is too much intellectual trifling and rhyming inanity, and here and there what the critics would denominate vapid sentiment.

If poetry is really "the bloom of high thought, the efflorescence of noble emotion", this kind of rattling versification does not indicate much elevation of thought and feeling among those who write and those who read. In some places it is even coarse, and everywhere it is wanting altogether in the calm restfulness of true art and that controlling mastery of the artist over his subject, which, indeed, bears the marks of spiritual excitement, but at the same time maintains a tone and manner which give dignity and distinction to noble ideas expressed in metre.

The following lines in "The Workman's Jubilee Ode" are not a fine specimen of cultured and refined humour:

> Hail, fiftieth year of sanctimonious robbery,
> Imperial brigandage, and licens'd crime;
> Religion mealy-mouthed, and cultured snobbery,
> And mawkish art and priggishness sublime!
> Hail, great Victorian age of cant and charity,
> When all are free, yet money-bags prevail;
> Huge Juggernaut of civilised barbarity,
> Lo! we, thy victims, bid thee hail, all hail!

Nor do the "Chants for Socialists" by the author of the "Earthly Paradise" impress us on the whole as worthy of their author's fame. We are disappointed by the want of force and fervour which we should expect here even from "the idle singer of an idle day" under the influence of the social passion, except, perhaps, in "The March of the Workers" where we hear as it were the stir and motion of marching "battalions of labour". And we are disappointed with the poems, as a whole, from an æsthetic point of view. Mr. Morris fails to strike the right note somehow, or the tone is not deep enough to inspire enthusiasm. In the "Message of the March Wind" we have elegiac reflectiveness and a hopeful tenderness which is touching without being disturbing, but it lacks vividness of emotion. There is about this and most of these laboured productions a kind of unconscious sense of failure and hopelessness of ever being able to touch the heart of the "British workman", that renders even this cunning artificer in rhyme feeble and uncertain, almost inefficient in his appeals.

In France, the land of "*Chants révolutionnaires*", the "*chanson social*" displays more fire and force than "sweetness and light". From the days of Chenier, Rouget de L'Isle, and Béranger, song has exercised a powerful influence on the people and stimulated the social-democratic movement, as did for example "*Le Chant des Ouvriers*", by Pierre Dupont in 1848. But if we except Eugène Pottier, whom Jules Vallés calls the Juvenal of the Faubourg and whom the "*Socialiste*", in its eulogy on the occasion of his demise in 1887, called the "Tyrtaeus of our labour party", there are few who have reached the heart of the French people as a whole. One or two excerpts from E. Pottier will show the drift and scope of his poetry. In the concluding apostrophe in "*Rêve du Forgeron*" we see the "scientific" bent of Pottier's socialism in verse

> "Toi, compagnon, prends ces outils qu'on nomme,
> *Raison, Progrès, Science, Égalité.*
> Sois plus qu'un roi, sois ton maître, sois homme:
> O travailleur, deviens Humanité."

We are reminded here of Walt Whitman's democratic

art. Other lines might be quoted in abundance in which science is represented as the power which shall demolish finally the capitalist, the soldier, and the priest, the ermined judge, and the rest, or where the ancient Communard poet, as in "*On fusille les Voleurs*", pronounces sentences of death on all the propertied classes. Throughout, as in "*Le quatrième État*" the material delights of the coming millennium are painted in sufficiently satiated colours; in them the famishing and ragged dwellers of the Faubourgs are promised mainly unstinted meals, a full plate, and flowing cup, as in the following:

> "Alors, abolissons les classes,
> Partageons devoirs et plaisirs;
> Reposez-vous, épaules lasses,
> Le vapeur vous fait des loisirs;
> La matière entre dans sa gloire:
> Nous mangeons tous au même plat;
> Et Pantagruel verse à boire
> Au quatrième état."

Not a very high poetic flight this! Truly it is a faithful French version of Lassalle's saying that the labour question is a question for the stomach. But such a theme lends itself better for treatment in prose.

Here we may quote the words of a writer in the *Revue Socialiste* for December 1891 on the functions of art. They serve as an apt criticism on the actual art of socialistic poetry and a criterion of what it ought to be. "Il faut une âme," says Georges Beaume. "Il faut une "conception de la vie, une foi, l'inquiétude d'un au-delà "terrestre. Il faut se jeter tout entier, capable de souffrir "et d'aimer, dans les angoisses et les aspirations du "temps, dont nous pouvons être une parole. Nous aurons "la joie de l'effort, la joie sainte du sacrifice et du "devoir, la folie des chimères. Nous aurons peut-être "l'illusion d'embrasser le monde et de l'emporter dans le "soleil vers les justices sublimes."

All this is really directed against the art and literature of the *Bourgeoisie*. But it is applicable to socialist poetry as well.

Here, however, it may be stated that it is premature to expect the highest efforts of poetry and still less of the Drama from a vast body of men such as the socialists, high and low, in their present position of militant excitement, engaged as they are in a fierce class struggle. It is in times of conscious greatness after conquests achieved, as in the days of Pericles, or in the Italian towns of the Renaissance and England under Queen Elizabeth that Art and the Drama flourished. It is a fair argument for socialists to say: when *we* have conquered, and have been delivered from the tyranny of artificial famine which now hinders the restful cultivation of art, we, too, shall win the laurels of poetic genius and shall enrich the world with a grand and noble literature; when we shall be put in a position to live a life worthy of human beings, and shall be enabled to develop our faculties without stint as to time and opportunity, when we shall all be invested with the full rights of free citizenship and shall have ceased to be engaged in the sordid struggles for mere existence we, too, shall create new ideals and live up to them, and our artists, poets and painters, architects and artificers in the plastic arts, and cunning handlers in all sorts of instruments of music will fill the world with sights and sounds which shall provide spiritual delights and perpetual feasts of reason in the society of the future.

An independent witness and competent critic in a

high-class German periodical tells us that the new epoch inaugurated by socialism is really an attempt to translate into fact the partly understood ideals of the last century. Then the subjective development of the individual was the end aimed at, now the great object is to apply the æsthetical and philosophical ideal to practical everyday life. Since this is possible only when ample provision is made for a material basis, bodily must precede intellectual development, and therefore the aim of the socialist movement is by means of material improvement to make the realization of the Ideal possible for the mass of the people. For this reason so far from being an obstacle to the rising up of a new art it will advance it. Unlike the now dominant principles of Art, those of the art of the future will be founded in nature, the new Art, like the giant Antæus, receives its force from mother Earth, having positive fact for its firm foundation.

CHAPTER VIII.

SOCIALISM AND ROMANISM.

> Léo XIII... a fait trois grandes choses, dont la première conséquence, a été de rendre au Catholicisme, et généralement à la religion, leur part d'action sociale.
>
> F. BRUNETIÈRE.
> *Revue des deux Mondes.*

> "Le labarum moderne, celui qui symbolise les espérances et les droits de l'humanité n'est plus à Rome. Depuis la Révolution française, le signe de la Croix ne peut plus être le signe de l'idéal nouveau. Le labarum contemporain est incontestablement le drapeau rouge.   A. VEBER.
> *Revue Socialiste.*

A SURVEY of Socialism in relation to modern thought would be incomplete without dwelling in the concluding chapters on the relation of modern religious thought in its two main branches to Socialism, and it will be understood that it is in this and no other sense that we use the terms Romanism and Protestantism. Among the many and costly presentations made at the Vatican on the occasion of the Pope's Jubilee a few years ago, none, probably, was more valued than that of the King of Saxony. It consisted of the *Biblia Pauperum* in facsimile, and contained a graceful inscription alluding to the successful efforts of Leo XIII in bringing home to the poor the blessings of the Gospel. This really was an allusion to those attempts at social amelioration in the Roman Church which have received in a marked degree the countenance of its present head, who, even as Cardinal Pecci, and almost as soon as he was called to the priesthood, turned his attention to questions of social interest. In his papal allocutions and other public utterances, Leo XIII. has more than once given expression to deep solicitude for the welfare of the working-classes in their present struggles, notably so on the occasion of receiving a body of French operatives, who had made a pilgrimage to Rome, and who, on being introduced to His Holiness by the general secretary of "*L'Œuvre des Cercles Catholiques d'Ouvriers*", heard the following words addressed to them in excellent French:—

"Nous mêmes, dès le début de notre pontificat, nous "avons pensé à vous, quand nous rappelions aux peuples " les principes fondamentaux de l'ordre social. Nous avons "suivi depuis, avec attention, les travaux des congrès tenu "successivement en France, en Italie, en Allemagne, et, " dans les derniers jours, en Belgique, et en Suisse; et nous " ne cesserons de faire, pour l'amélioration de votre sort, " tout ce que notre charge et notre coeur de Père pourront "nous suggérer."

A superficial observer might be inclined to think that nothing but antagonism could exist between two such movements as Socialism and Romanism. But a little reflection will soon discover causes of mutual attraction even in their fundamental theories of society. Both are international and cosmopolitan, aiming at universality, patriotism and nationality occupying at least a secondary place in either system. Both attach supreme importance to association and organisation under a centralized government, though under very different kinds of rulers. Both prefer regulated co-operation and the corporate forms of Industry to competition and individual enterprise, one tending towards the Commune as the type of social union in the future, the other to the *régime corporatif* as the typical form of the organization of labour in the past. Both are, therefore, alike opposed to the principle of *laisser-faire, laisser-aller*, and the results of that system in the establishment of *bourgeois* predominancy, or middle-class rule during the last hundred years. Both tend towards a levelling uniformity, though social inequalities within given limits are fully recognized by Romanists and in a manner so decided as to provoke the most hostile criticism of Socialists. Both are frequently brought into conflict with Governments on account of their anarchical and hierarchical tendencies respectively. These are some of the points of contact. There are also fundamental differences, producing mutual repulsion. They disagree in their views as to the basis on which the social edifice rests, and the means and methods of social amelioration. According to "the Socialist heresy" the will of the "sovereign people" forms the keystone of the society. According to the Roman conception, it is founded on Divine authority, that authority being represented visibly by the "sovereign Pontiff". Socialism comes into conflict with Romanism, moreover, by its negation of the sacredness of marriage, and its tendency to destroy the bonds of family life, and also its virtual denial of the rights of private property. Its revolutionary methods of social reconstruction, which would break with the past, entirely clash with the Roman conception of historical continuity. Its impatience with the existing social order, and its scornful disregard of religious consolation under privations and trials, are little to the taste of "Social Catholics", who are as anxious to "repress insatiable egotism" among those in possession, "which so much lowers and enfeebles human nature", as it is opposed to the rapacity of those who, to use the words of the Encyclical, "aim at seizing and holding in common whatever has been acquired by the title of lawful inheritance, or by the intellect or labour of the hands, or by frugal living". In the latest Encyclical, indeed, we read that "the impartiality of the law and the true brotherhood of men were first asserted by Jesus Christ". But, then, one of the most pronounced of Catholic Christian Socialists explains that the guiding principle of that brotherhood must be "le dévouement s'exerçant à l'ombre de la croix".

In fact, Romanism regards both Socialism and Individualism—which latter it is in the habit of identifying with Continental Liberalism—as the "frères ennemis", both anti-Christian in their nature, but its natural antipathies towards the latter, apart from other reasons to be mentioned farther on, incline it to greater sympathy with the former.

This new Catholic movement must be, therefore, carefully distinguished from that of the Liberal Catholics, such as Lamennais and his school of some fifty years ago. It calls itself Catholic-Conservative, and its representatives mainly belong to the *élite* of society, clerical and lay. Not only in France, but in all European countries with large Roman Catholic populations, especially in Austria, its leaders at this present moment aim at no less than a counter-revolution to undo the effects wrought by the first French Revolution. French writers of this school even suggest that the thread of social development must be taken up again where it was snapped asunder by the Revolution coming in as a disturbing factor in the even progress of social evolution and reform, *i.e.* at the stage immediately preceding the *ancien régime* which was itself too much under the influence of the eighteenth century philosophy, *i.e.* before the breaking up of the institutions bequeathed to society by Mediævalism. Thus, it is hoped, the mental, moral, and social anarchy resulting from the Rationalism of the revolutionary period, coinciding with the rule of *laissez-faire* in Economics, will be replaced by a new order which will bring peace at the last.

"A cette *anarchie* libérale et révolutionnaire, il faut, sous "peine d'être bientôt jété par le courant dans l'abîme du "Socialisme démocratique, où s'engloutirait tout ce qui reste "encore d'ordre social, il faut, dis-je, opposer la *hiérarchie*," which consists in "*la distribution harmonieuse et ordon-"née des différents groupes de la société, d'après les fonctions "naturelles et sociales, qui leur sont propres, sous la direction "de l'autorité.*" *

This suggests a two-fold inquiry. (1) How do the accredited teachers of Romanism account for the rise of Social Democracy; and having traced it to its source historically, (2) how do they propose to direct its course? In other words, what are the regulating and restricting forces called into requisition in order to conduct the Socialistic movement into safe channels, according to the lessons of past experience?

* "*Révolution et Evolution—Le Centenaire de 1789, et les Conservateurs Catholiques*", par G. de Pascal, Paris, 1888. pp. 67 and *ante*.

In their historical criticism, Romanist critics display a characteristic skill in logical fence, in their endeavour to strike a double blow at the Reformation and the Revolution, in making them conjointly responsible for the evils of Capitalism and Socialism. They agree with Karl Marx in calling Luther the progenitor of Capitalism, while Individualism, the child of Protestantism, is the parent of modern Industrialism. In the same way Socialists speak of Protestantism as the "religion of private property", or "the religion of the *bourgeoisie*", whilst both Socialists and Romanists dwell with bitter irony on the effects of that social revolution which made the pursuit of private interest and free competition the rule of life in modern industry. The Reformation and the Revolution thus having failed to satisfy the friends and enemies of the present social order, what remains but to look for social reforms to another quarter, hence the demand for "*une sérieuse et salutaire réaction*".

It is curious to find that Proudhon, in his "Confessions of a Revolutionary", published in 1880, comes from his Socialistic, or rather Anarchist, standpoint to the same conclusion, though it is not hard to guess which of the two alternatives he prefers.

"Le moment", he says, "est donc venu pour les puis-
"sances de l'Europe ou de s'abjurer elles-mêmes devant
"l'interrogation des citoyens, ou de rappeler les Jésuites
"et de restaurer le Pape".

Here Socialism and Romanism part company. The Social Democracy cannot go back. For them the French Revolution is only the precursor of the Social Revolution that is to be. The descendants of the men of '89 care little for the Reformation of the sixteenth century; nay, in a measure, they share the antipathy of Romanists against it, but they also remind the representatives of Catholic reaction that the agrarian revolts of the Reformation period were nothing else but attempts to shake off the fetters of the feudal *régime* for which the Roman Church was in a measure responsible, and to which now she expresses a desire to return. They also point out that the excesses of the Reign of Terror were the outburst of popular wrath against social oppression supported by religious terrorism for centuries. The clerical counter-revolution, they add, is nothing else but an attempt to restore the social caste-system under priestly rule which prevailed in the dark ages, or something much akin to it, a " Communism of Papal Theocracy".

It is always best to accept in their own words the definition of those concerned as to the actual standpoint they occupy. We will do so in this instance. Le Comte de Mun speaks as the mouth-piece of the Social Catholics, and his character and position leave no doubt as to the sincerity and accuracy of his statements. He belongs to an old and noble French family; his father's mother traced her origin to James I. He also belongs to the aristocracy of talent, his great-grandfather having married a daughter of Helvetius. His own mother, Eugènie de la Ferronays, is mentioned in Madame Craven's *Récit d'une Sœur*, and through her the relations of his family with Lamennais, Lacordaire, Montalembert, and Bishop Gerbet probably gave the first impulse to his own social Catholic sympathies. He was intended, like many distinguished members of his family, for military service, and had his own share in the war with Germany, being one of the prisoners at the fall of Metz, but it was "in the face of the flames of the Paris Commune" that he vowed to become "an apostle of labour". He began to visit the chief centres of industry and to organize the labourers, giving up his military career to devote himself entirely to the work of social regeneration and re-organization. He became the founder and general secretary of the *Œuvre des Cercles Catholiques d'Ouvriers*, as well as a member of the House of Deputies, and in this two-fold capacity he has had ample opportunities of giving expression to the opinion of the party whom he leads. In one of his stirring speeches, delivered ten years ago, on the occasion of a pilgrimage to the Church of Notre Dame at Chartres on the part of the Catholic workmen's clubs connected with the *Œuvre*, and in answer to the question, "Are we Socialists?" he says:—

"No! no! we are not, and never will be Socialists. "Socialism is the negation of Divine authority which we "affirm, and is the affirmation of man's absolute indepen- "dence which we deny; it is the passion of possession, "and our doctrine is founded on renunciation. Socialism "is the logical outcome of the Revolution; there is there- "fore nothing in common between us."

But again addressing himself to the general body of this society at the closing of its anniversary meeting in 1882, he says:—

"If it is being a Socialist to be anxious to secure for "the labourer what is his due, to see that the conditions "of liberty are regulated in such a way so as to prevent "his becoming the victim of competition in spite of "himself, to prevent his wife from deserting her home for "the factory and the workshop, to prevent his children "from doing work at an age too tender, exposing body

"and mind to premature decay; if to make sure that self-
"interest shall not be the only measure of estimating the
"value of work done, that the workman shall recover in
"his Sunday rest the moral and material guarantees of
"that independence which the Church had secured for
"him so that he shall be enabled gradually to rise in
"his profession—if to wish for all this is being a
"Socialist, I can understand why we are accused of being
"that.... No, gentlemen, we are not, and we never
"shall be Socialists; we want the solution of the social
"question, that is all, and this solution we expect from
"the Christian Tradition."

Such is the position of what we may call the *avant-garde* of the movement. We may proceed in the next place to consider the actual opinions of the accredited representatives of Romanism on such burning questions as the relations of capital and labour, the respective merits of Individualism and Socialism, the much discussed question of self-help and State-help for the protection of labour, and the promotion of associative modes of industry as a means of counteracting the evils of individual isolation.

To begin with the relation of capital and labour: Here it will be interesting to note not only what economic theorists and clerical or clerically-minded philanthropists have to say on the subject, but also how far they are seconded by practical business men and by lay employers of labour of the Roman Communion.

Both Dr. Ratzinger, in his work on Political Economy, founded on ethics, and Canon Hitze, as the general secretary of the *Arbeiterwohl* (corresponding to the French

Œuvre) as well as a Deputy of the Prussian Landtag and German Diet, in his lectures on Capital and Labour and the Reorganization of Society, establish a claim which few would call in question, that the Roman Church in her monastic discipline, including manual labour, as in the case of the monks of St. Bernard in particular, and in the teachings of her great mediæval revivalists, such as St. Francis, "the ardent lover of poverty", has pronouncedly accentuated the duty and dignity of labour. To the organization of the guilds and labour corporations of the same period, under the fostering care of the Church, they ascribe the growth of those two modern ideas, the "liberty of labour" and the "rights of labour", as well as the prosperity and progress of industry before the era of manufacture and machinery. They point out the contrast between the cordial co-operation of those engaged in the trades then, including masters, journeymen, and apprentices, mostly living under the same roof and partaking of the common meal at the same table, and in happy harmony applying their common skill to the production of articles of use, and the unhappy divisions of employers now with the separation of interests resulting from the division of labour in the present modes of industry. For in producing all commodities, not for immediate customers but for the market, modern industry separates producers and consumers as well as employers and employed.

To this disintegrating principle of modern Commercialism they ascribe the unhappy divorce of the manual producer from the instruments of production, and his consequent dependence on capital, *i.e.*, capitalist employers, which is in contradiction to the formal freedom he enjoys in the eyes of the law, and to the political liberty, which is the outcome of the same commercial era (for the French Revolution and the Revolution of Industry coincide in point of time and aims). Practically, they say, the worker must sell his work for what it can fetch in the wages market, and the purchaser of it becomes the sole owner of his labour for the time being. Labour thus is degraded into a mere link or pivot in the mechanism of production. The relation between the recipient of wages and his employer ceases to be personal; he has sunk into the position of a commodity. The sole aim of production now is simply profit, and everything else is of subordinate importance:—

"Millions, even myriads, are thus amassed (says Ratzinger) by means of impoverished labourers selling their work for a song among the agricultural and factory populations of Great Britain and Ireland, on which hangs the curse of the disinherited, who, on account of the over-powering predominance of capital have never received the full value of the work done by them."

The iron law of wages prevails, indeed, not because it is an actual law of nature, but a practical abuse of power on the part of the stronger. If in this matter capitalists were guided by the principles of moral law, the fate of those who depend on them would be better than it is, but individual employers are powerless in competing with the rest. Here, then, the community, through the State, must come to the rescue, and protect man against iron necessity from without. Public authority must be paramount over the "authority of competition", and restore order in the chaos of conflicting interests, so that the higher interests of the community may be protected against the interests of private cupidity. "Employers of labour", supplements Hitze, in a later pamphlet on this subject, "must render the path of legislation easy, and cheerfully second the efforts of social politicians".

But more than this is wanted. There are times when to go back is the best way of advancing. We are living in such times, and, as a matter of fact, the loudest laudators of modern progress are retrogressive in this respect, that they return to heathenish methods of avaricious exactions against which the Church set her face in the ages of faith; exactions, moreover, which brought ruin eventually on the culture and civilization of the Roman Empire. As Christianity rescued that society from complete annihilation in regenerating it, so now, by means of a return to Christian methods of industry, the formation of Christian institutions for mutual succour and support, and the organization of associations of production in one form or another, the work of social reconstruction can alone be effected.

What is wanted is a widely-extended system of "Patronage", *i.e.* something like a restitution of the patriarchal relationship between master and man, and a reunion of the men themselves in corporations of the several trades and branches of industry to which they are attached; in short, a serious attempt has become imperative to re-collect the units of our "pulverized society" into something corresponding to the Christian ideas of union and communion, so utterly at variance with the individualist tendencies of the day. This attempt at reunion, says Ratzinger, is the only demand which Socialism and Romanism have in common, as also it is the only part of the Socialistic programme which has any chance of realization. But, he adds, Romanism differs from Socialism in this respect, that it rejects the doctrine of absolute equality in each of the units thus to be reorganized, since humanity can never consist of equal atoms or simple ciphers, a graduated scale in rank and social subordination being essential to its nature. The higher the organism, adds Hitze, the greater will be this kind of differentiation. But Socialism and Romanism differ still more in the methods of their reorganization, the former tending downwards in resorting to compulsion, and aiming at the satisfaction of personal desire; the latter tending upwards, through self-reliance and self-denial, through love and liberty to work out a higher social destiny.

Thus, generally speaking, the Roman Church as the *Mater dolorosa*, in her anxiety to ease the sufferings of the poor, may be compared to the courageous mother who confronted the lion with her child between its teeth, attacking "*la liberté féroce de la concurrence*", to prevent the lion's share of profit being taken from her children. Antipathy towards the unbelieving capitalist may add fuel to her just anger, but there can be no doubt as to its sincerity. Prejudice may obscure the judgment at times, so as to prevent the zealous controversialist from distinguishing as carefully as might be wished between liberty and license, egoism and egoistic unfairness, unfettered and unprincipled competition. This is natural enough. Personal prepossessions affect the judgment. Rome represents law and order. The principle of *laissez faire* leads to economic anarchy, for in the absence of ethic restraints in the competition struggle, the law of the strongest is apt to prevail. The Liberal Economist allows of no other but the laws of nature in the play of economic forces, the Roman Economist refers everything to the laws of the Church, "*l'ordre où régnent le droit et le devoir.*"

On some points Romanist writers and speakers differ, and we must devote the concluding portion of this chapter to the discussion of one of them *i.e.* the province of the State, or the social politics of Vaticanism.

Two fundamental faults are pointed out by Hitze which it is the duty of the State to remedy in the "capitalistic order of society".

(1.) Its defective methods of production and distribution.

(2.) The want of unity of plan in the process of production.

That process is mechanical, excluding personal relationship between the directing minds and the manual labourers engaged in it, and it is carried on without concerted action among the producing firms; hence the evil of overproduction. What is therefore wanted is more public control of the process of production, to protect the weak, and public measures for supplementing what is lacking in the present modes of production, with a view to introduce some kind of order into the present chaos. The solution of the Social problem consists in the replacing of Individualism by Socialism, the atomizing process of competition by solidarity, mechanical combination by personal bonds. In the place of this anarchy of production, we want order, instead of the expropriation of the weak by the strong, the strengthening of the weak and the curbing of the strong, and in the place of individual independence, the subordination of the individual to the educated moral sense of the community. What is essential is the restoration of the rights of society over the individual and capital. In the concrete, society may act through, as it is represented by, the corporation and the

State. It may be dangerous to invest an Autocratic State with these powers, but order has it claims as well as liberty. Such are the sentiments almost literally transcribed from Hitze's work on "Capital and Labour", written in 1881, and dated, as we observe in the preface, from the German Campo Santo in Rome, where the distance from the centre of Imperial power, perhaps, added to the sense of security from the abuses of power; but in the worst cases, he says, even State Socialism is better than Capitalism.

Some explanation, however, is required of the fact that the progress of Social Reform is so tardy in Belgium, even when an Ultramontane Government is in power, and yet this is the charge preferred by Roman Catholics, notably the late leader of the Social Catholic party in Austria. Perhaps, if we turn our attention to this latter country it will throw further light on the subject.

Here, in the last and strongest bulwark of Conservatism, in a country to a great extent agricultural, a country, too, grown rich since 1848 by the spread of varied industries, economic Liberalism and anti-clerical Josephenism form the most formidable opponents to Romanism. Here, too, "the experts of Anarchy" are drawn up in full battle array against what remains of Autocratic rule, though Sir Charles Dilke is probably exaggerating in saying that "Socialism is perhaps a greater and more present danger in the Dual Monarchy than in any other country". In Austria-Hungary, Liberalism is mainly represented by the Jewish *bourgeoisie,* which "is barked at by anti-Semitic dogs, and howled at by democratic wolves". It is here that we find the Catholic Social party advancing at full speed. State Socialism is called by the Baron von Vogelsang:—

"A grand educational measure for which humanity
"ought to be grateful, and which history will crown with
"an unfading garland of glory." Better than the "omnipotence of the plutocratic State" is the "omnipotence of
the princely patriarchal State of even the pigtail period."
"All ways lead to Rome. Socialism, too, will be led in
"that direction, provided that in the counsels of God there
"is a future for Europe, worthy of human destiny.... In
"their critical views, materialistic Social Democrats and
"Christians often run on parallel lines. 'Property is theft'
"is a Christian and social truth if the modern explanation
"of property is accepted as absolute property, unconditioned
"by political and social duties. The use of private property,
"on the principle that we can do what we like with it,
"is robbery of that which belongs to God, Society and
"the State." *

What follows but that the State must step in and
vindicate its just claims and those of Society; the Church
will take care of the things which belong to God.

In Austria, then, where Roman Catholicism is strong
in the Court and aristocratic circles, and through them
able to counteract the influence of plutocracy in the
legislature, State Socialism in the form of paternal Government
finds its most powerful advocates, whilst such proposals
as those of the Liberal member Plener for the representation
of labour in the form of an "Arbeiter Kammer" to
supplement the actual delegation by orders actually existing

* See *Gesummelte Aufsätze über socialpolitische und verwandte
Themata*, von Freiherr C. von Vogelsang. Heft. iv, pp. 216—18; Heft.
vii. pp. 389—92. It is the party formerly led by this sturdy representative of State Socialism which has become so formidable of late, a
rather inconvenient ally, and a still more inconvenient antagonist of
State Authority.

already, receives but scant support from the Social Catholics and their organs in the Press, though they, like the rest, insist on the creation of corporate organizations as the best means of solving the Social Question.

Metternich, writing in 1840 to the Marquis de Saint-Aulaire on the revolutionary decomposition of society in France, said, "Les bons esprits en France ne trouveront le ciment propre à la réconstruction de l'édifice sociale que dans la voix de la Corporation," and Catholics in that country were engaged in celebrating the centenary in 1889 by a systematic refutation of "the false dogmas of 1789".

We may touch on one or two points in the social policy of the party led by the Comte de Mun in that country, and contrast it with the attitude of the Social Catholics in Germany, thus completing our survey, and drawing, or rather help our readers in drawing their own conclusion.

During the Debate in the French Chamber on the Insurance against Accidents Law, on the 28th May, 1888, and the Law for the Protection of Women and Children on the 11th of June in the following year the Comte de Mun delivered two speeches which sufficiently indicate the drift of social politics of the party he represents. After speaking of the evils of the constant conflicts of private interests in which the weak go to the wall, and the social dilemma between the pulverizing effects of individualism and the centralizing effects of bureaucracy, he says the only remedy is State intervention:

"To remedy this and to counteract its effects, there "is but one means, if possible worse than the disease, "namely the ever-growing intervention of the State; we "must say outright, State Socialism, to the legal organisation

"of which we are proceeding every day with giant strides.
"Anarchy and State Socialism—those are the two necessary
"and inevitable terms of the individualist system of which
"the modern economic *régime* consists."

This being the case, all social laws must have for their object the restitution of labour, now degraded into merchandise, to its former honourable position and dignity. And as the law then under discussion would have a binding power in associating those for whose benefit it would be passed, it would amount to State recognition of the desirability of forming those "corps autonomes" from the organization of which Catholics in all European countries expect so much. It would be a step towards "*l'organisation d'institutions professionelles basée sur la solidarité*". The two reasons given by the Comte de Mun in support of the law for protecting women and children, and as an excuse for his becoming a "*partisan de la réglementation du travail*", are, again (1) that work is a public function, (2) because the principal mission of the State power is to be the guardian of justice and the protector of all, especially of the most feeble; for as he says, quoting Lacordaire: "*Entre le fort et le faible c'est la liberté qui opprime, et c'est la loi qui affranchit.*"

Of course he speaks here of the function of Government in the abstract; for the present Government in France the Count and his followers have no other feeling but that of pronounced antagonism. "*Le Parlementarisme voilà l'ennemi!*" was the challenge thrown at them in the Romans' speech, in reply to Gambetta's *mot*, "*le Cléricalisme voilà l'ennemi!*" But there is no reason why he should not smite his enemies with their own weapons, driving out Satan by Beelzebub, and using the prevailing form of State legislation for the purpose of striking a blow at the system by which it exists. When the reporter of the Commission, during the debate on the subject referred to, interrupted the Comte de Mun in his speech, reminding him in the House that the real intentions of the speaker, as stated before the Commission, were to call into existence a number of Catholic corporations, holding property and legal status under the existing law of Syndicate, and thus to spread a net of Catholic associations over the whole country, the Comte de Mun admitted this, indeed, to be his pious wish, and that from its fulfilment he expected real social peace. But, in the meantime, he would accept less, and what will ultimately lead to it.

This, too, in general, is the course adopted by the Centre party in the German Diet, but with a difference. The work of association and organization has been going on here vigorously, and more successfully than elsewhere ever since 1848, when "Piusvereine" were formed under Ketteler's directions, and "Gesellenvereine" under Kolping. After the short episode of Ronge's "German Catholicism", which converted his congregations into Radical clubs in strong sympathy with the Communist tendencies of the times, attempts have been made to establish some kind of link between Romanism and Radicalism similar to that aimed at in 1830, and again in 1848 in France. But the object is not to radicalize Romanism, but to romanize Radicalism. Association and organization on Catholic principles further this end. These associations are to enjoy State protection. But State Socialism is approached with more caution by the responsible leaders of Catholic opinion, and by the central organ of Catholic social reform in Germany, whilst the opinions of Hitze and others referred to above are only endorsed with careful qualification on this head. Not many years ago a number of articles appeared in the *Christlich-Sociale Blätter* under the title " A Momentous Decision", referring to the final verdict on the Bill to ensure the labourer against the effects of old age and infirmity which was finally passed on the 24th of May 1889, and that only with the help of a minority of the Centre party who voted in favour of the measure in spite of its warnings against the tendency of increasing too much the influence of Bureaucracy. "In accepting the principle that it is right to use public funds in the interest of one social class, and in pursuance of a particular policy of State, and to give effect to it by compulsion, this is a new departure in legislation; it amounts to a legal proclamation of State Socialism in its most pronounced form." " Here we stand," we read farther on, "on the cross-roads where Christian-Social and State-Socialist policies part company." "It amounts to a *triumph of the Socialist idea*", and *the complete isolation of the Church* and her unchangeable opposition to the party of social subversion."

Here, then, Romanism, pitted against Protestant Cæsarism in the plentitude of its power, is less inclined to invoke State aid than in France, where it finds itself face to face with a weakened and discredited Government, atheistic in spirit, and as such in antagonism with the general tone of religious feeling in a catholic country, where the cry " *Chasse aux prêtres* " has found no echo, but has strengthened rather than weakened the party of Catholic Reaction.

This, then, is the result of our enquiry, that, whilst the whole course and tendency in the special policy of Romanism leaves no doubt as to its sincerity in sympathizing with the more moderate demands of Social Democracy, it is equally certain by its own confession, that the great aim of this policy is the weakening of the *bourgeoisie,* and the ultimate destruction, if possible, of the liberal *régime.* Open war is declared against individualism, and so far, Romanism moves on parallel lines with Socialism. For this reason the demand for State-Socialism is most pronounced in Austria, where it affords the best means for frightening the *bourgeoisie,* and least so in Germany, where the State is both willing and powerful enough to do this on its own account, to the detriment of Church influence, especially in Prussia, where, since 1809 the Catholic Church has been regarded in the light of a State institution, and her priesthood as State officials. For this reason the demand for State interference is more pronounced in France at the present political juncture, where the State may be used and used up without danger for social purposes, strengthening rather than weakening the ecclesiastical position. It is more cautious in Belgium— cautious to a fault as we saw—where the State engine, under a Liberal Constitution, and in the presence of political equilibrium of power equally divided, and shared alternately by the Ultramontanes and Liberals, might be used by the latter as well as the former for their own advantages when in office. That ecclesiastical ascendency, *pro majore gloria Dei,* is kept in view in all these moves of social policy is natural enough. It is not so much as denied by those concerned, though made too much of, and sometimes unfairly misrepresented by adversaries, as when one of them, speaking of the double-mindedness of Romanism asserts that the Pope condemns every form of **extra**-Catholic Socialism, whilst at the same time cultivating most assiduously that which may be considered as intra-Catholic, trying to turn socialistic influence in the bulk of the population to his own account. Other churches might learn a lesson of *savoir-faire* from the Church of Rome, either as a Church of Opportunism or a Church in Opposition, namely, not to leave a nerve unstrained to make their spiritual power felt among the masses, and to take care not to alienate, but to lead rather than vainly try to resist the onward march of democracy. Claiming, as the Church of Rome does, to be not only the sole depository of Divine truth, but also the "guardian of all *Social* truth", what more natural than that she should endeavour to emphasize by all means in her power that social doctrine which she believes to be the only true doctrine. A strong belief in their own sacred mission is an essential factor of success in ecclesiastical organizations for those who have the good of the people at heart, though they take not their stand on the axiomatic assertion "*extra ecclesiam nulla salus*" in matters social or religious. It is quite open to other religious bodies to reject such claims on the part of one branch of the Church Catholic, and the present writer has no desire or vocation to make himself the champion of such unwarrantable assumption. He merely states the case without defending or controverting the position taken up by those whose policy he describes. At the same time, viewing the matter from his own standpoint, studying the social question and the subject of socialism in their relation to one of the greatest religious forces on the present day, as one among many modes of thought, and tracing thus the connection between Socialism and Romanism, and not writing here as a religious controversialist, he cannot help making considerable allowance for earnest men not of his own Communion, and giving them full credit for their good intentions. He cannot withhold his respectful sympathy from a Romanist writer who, in his tractate on "The Social-Political Importance and Activity of the Holy Father Leo XIII", makes the following assertion:—

"Christian Society, above all things, must be reorganized "according to God's will, recommencing actively its course "according to the divine plan. This must be its heart "and centre if those social maladies are to cease against "which we are fighting."

The heart and centre may not be in Rome or Geneva, not in this or that local branch of the Church of Christ; but it is wherever Christianity exists as a spiritual force, and the Christian Church as a spiritual organization. Religion is the soul of social organisms, the formative principle working from within; therefore, to use the words of the great social reformer, Le Play, "Let us place Society anew under the guardian protection of religious faith".

CHAPTER IX

SOCIALISM AND PROTESTANTISM

> "Jedenfalls ist das Geburtsland der modernen Social-Demokratie die Welt des Protestantismus." THEODOR ARNDT.
>
> "Die wirthschaftlichen Ziele, denen die Arbeiter unter Führung der Socialdemokratie zustreben, im Namen der christlichen Kirche zu bekämpfen, sind unchristlich."
> *Resolutions passed at the 2nd Evangelical Social Congress in Berlin 1891.*

PROTESTANTISM, says Karl Marx in his *Capital*, is essentially a bourgeois religion. His followers in England and America explain this further by saying that from its religious Individualism follows in a direct line economic Liberalism which is the bugbear of Socialism, that from the Protestant principle of liberty of conscience is derived the doctrine of natural liberty, the parent of *laissez-faire* in Economics, *i.e.* freedom of contract and unlimited competition, whence they affirm flow all the evils complained of in our modern social system, and that as a matter of fact it is in Protestant countries that capitalism chiefly prevails.

"The predominately commercial States of Christendom are the predominately Protestant ones, while even in Catholic Countries the main strength of the Protestant minority lies in the trading classes." * E. de Laveleye, Alexis de

* E. Belfort Bax: "The Religion of Socialism", p. 77 and also compare *Revue Socialiste* for April 1890, p. 409—10.

Tocqueville and M. Guizot, J. E. Thorold Rogers, F. Seebohm and many other well-known writers at home and abroad say the same, but they consider that this rather redounds to the glory of Protestantism as an Economic force, inasmuch as what we call modern progress is mainly the result of the enterprise and industry consequent upon the liberation of mind in the 16th century. Even a leading German Protestant divine, addressing himself to the task of comparing the social and economic influences of Romanism and Protestantism respectively, admits this, and asserts with pride that "the machine is somewhat in the nature of Protestantism".* But it is the division of work by machine labour as a source of wealth to some, which enslaves and impoverishes man as an appendage of the labour-saving machine, says the modern Socialist, as, indeed, did the Protestant economist Sismondi in his day. Moreover, adds our Socialist critic of modern industry, thus conducted it is the theory of the sacredness of private property first formulated by Grotius and other Protestant legists, and the Egotism praised as an economic virtue in the 17th and 18th centuries and canonized as a creed by the orthodox economists following the Scotch Protestant Adam Smith, which let loose on the world all the unbridled forces of Industrial competition and conflict, the passionate desire for accumulating wealth and the various methods of increasing profits at the expense of the labourers, which has brought about the present situation. Even Doellinger traced pauperism as the companion of progress in England to the Reformation, and in this way the bad effects of the prevailing industrial system are by many unimpassioned

* "Katholicismus und Protestantismus gegenüber der sozialen Frage", von Gerhard Uhlhorn, 1887.

and impartial writers on the subject attributed to the economic effects of Protestantism.

It is well, therefore, before we speak of the present relations of Socialism and Protestantism to show what are the actual principles of Protestantism as far as they effect the social question, then to examine the relation of modern Protestant thought to socialistic theories, and lastly what is done and remains to be done in Protestant communities by way of practically solving the problem.

That Protestantism encourages the accumulation of Capital, and with Luther recommends the worthy use of temporal goods, that it encourages indirectly the pursuit of private interest, having regard to individual rather than collective advancement, is an undeniable fact. But it is not the Reformation alone which is answerable for this; it shares the responsibility with the movement of the Renaissance and the revival of natural science studies consequent upon discoveries coinciding in time, or nearly so, with the religious movement. These conjointly widened the minds of men. They brought together the literary treasures of Antiquity and the material wealth of the New World, stimulating human activity in all directions, naturally tending to commercial expansion, and gradually producing that regard for a "splendid materiality" and that peculiar "rage of ownership" which has, indeed, added much to the vigour of enterprise, although it has been to the great detriment of those who are left behind in the race after wealth. For a time, and to some extent even at the present moment, Protestantism leaning on the State has given some countenance to the competition of nations, and to "national egoism" in the industrial warfare of political economy. And here, again, Protestantism unlike Romanism, being national rather than international in its general tendencies, is more opposed to Socialism than its rival. But the Reformation and the Renaissance alike were a revolt against the mediæval ideas of terrestrial life, both encourage a healthy mundane philosophy which sanctions and stimulates human energy and effort in the affairs of this life with a view to healthy enjoyment. Reformers like Luther and typical humanists like Erasmus and Ulrich von Hutten, however, are opposed to the greed for wealth, and severely inveigh against commercial rapacity and luxurious indulgence. Wyclif stands up as the apostle of equality, discountenancing the oppressive measures of the craft guilds of his day. Nor should it be forgotten that in placing high honour on honest labour the Reformers did much towards emancipating it from existing civic disabilities and preparing the way for the modern vindication of its claims.* In this respect the Reformation supplemented the work left unfinished by the Renaissance, the classical ideal of free labour falling far below that of the Christian. Nor should it be forgotten that the theory of private property and the system stigmatized as "Capitalism" are derived from classical modes of thought, and from the re-introduction of Roman Law with the classical revival, rather than the influence of the Reformation. Thus it was, as the present writer has stated elsewhere,†

* In the "Adages" Erasmus applying the saying *A mortuo tributum exigere* to the acquisition of riches by unscrupulous means, says: "The rage of *ownership* has gone to such extremes that there is nothing in the world, sacred or profane, that is not beaten into money ..... and, what is most cruel of all, *the wretched common people are defrauded and their necessary food curtailed by innumerable tithes and taxes.*"—Drummond's "Life of Erasmus," Vol. I. p. 284.

† See Dictionary of Political Economy edited by R. H. Inglis

the combined influence of the spirit of curiosity in the age of the New Learning, with that of cupidity roused by the discoveries of gold in the New World and other sources of material aggrandizement, together with that of the contemporaneous religious liberation of the human mind, which led to the stupendous development of economic resources which forms the foundation of modern wealth and the hideous contrasts between progress and poverty. Nor should it be forgotten that Humanism, as the principle of cultivating man as man, blending with the Humanism in the sense of Christian Philanthropy, has ever since been developed into a system of ministering in a variety of ways to the weaknesses and necessities of human nature, so as to modify the hard inequalities entailed by free competition, and to lessen the evils of selfishness by the cultivation of human sympathy. In this way the supposed representative of pure egoism in political economy, Adam Smith, says, in the much decried "Wealth of Nations": "It is the industry which is carried on for the benefit of the rich and the powerful that is principally encouraged by our mercantile system"—and this he attacks. "That which is carried on for the benefit of the poor and indigent, is too often either neglected or oppressed." This he implicitly recommends. It is in Germany, the land of classical culture and prevailing Protestant thought, that the modern school of political economists arose who opposed with might and main the fallacy that political economy is simply the science of wealth, who have vindicated for it a place among the moral and historical

Palgrave, F.R.S. under heads *Christianity and Economics*, *The Influence of Protestant Thought on Economic Opinion and Practice;* and again under *Humanism, its Influence on Economics*.

sciences having for its object the welfare of humanity as a whole. It is in the latest and most authoritative German hand-book of the science that we are told its ethics are to teach "social man the duty of not only following egoistically his own interest, but also the welfare of others, and unselfishly to provide the community, according to his ability, with the requisites for the material and spiritual elevation of his fellows" whilst the State is defined as the grandest moral institution, bound to use its force in the pursuit of all economic interests, and by rational State-intervention to supplement the deficiencies of self-help. It is the Danish Protestant Bishop Martensen who appeals to the State to bring about "a just distribution of the common social products of all for all". In fact pages might be filled simply with the names and titles of productions by Protestant divines and laymen more or less distinguished, some holding the highest position in the Church and State, who give expression to similar sentiments, make positive proposals more or less defined to bridge over the gulf between riches and poverty, to restore labour to a place of dignity, to remove as far as possible the obstacles to its emancipation, to lift the masses materially, morally and mentally to a level with those classes who are now in full possession of all the means of wealth and comfort, in short to remodel society on the principle of Christian equality.

But a more plausible charge is preferred against Protestantism in a Roman Catholic brochure on the relation of Protestantism and Socialism. The author attributes to the individualizing tendencies of Protestantism the destruction of the social bonds which in the mediæval structure of society held together men in associations, trade-guilds, and other social and industrial institutions, but which the Reformation and its child the Revolution destroyed. Protestant Individualism, he says, is eventually subjectivism, egoism: for this very reason, he adds, it prepared a way for Radical Socialism and Communism, the one extreme producing its opposite. We are quite ready to admit that the germ of social disintegration is contained in Individualism, *i.e.* Individualism unmodified by any counteracting influences. But we cannot admit that the principles of the Reformation exclude that which M. Guizot has claimed for Christianity, *i.e.* the *fécond principe d'association* which re-collected the scattered elements of Roman society at its dissolution. On the contrary, A. de Tocqueville shows how in the United States the growth of commercial associations is a sign of the power of free associations taught by Protestantism, and that in democratic countries—and America owes its democratic constitution to its Puritan settlers—"la Science de l'association est la *science mère*", to which it might be added that the various attempts at co-operation and free combination, as in trades unions in recent times, have most signally prospered in Protestant countries. These are the antidotes of competition and the best available means for mutual protection and support among those least able to hold their own in the competitive struggle, as also they are the best means of bringing about a more evenly diffused distribution of economic productions.

But we must not be lured away into controversy about abstract principles and their tendencies. It will be more to the point to shew what is being said and done by some modern representatives of Protestantism by way of settling the social question, or by way of meeting socialist demands. Take for example the following paragraphs extracted from the Resolutions passed at the 4th General Assembly of the Evangelical Union in Stuttgart a few years ago: under head No. 5, *referring to Associations of Labourers* we read, "The Fourth General Assembly of the Evangelical Alliance expresses its cheerful adhesion to the efforts for the formation of Evangelical Labour Associations in Germany and urgently calls upon all local unions and their members to invite the labourers to join associations for the purpose of raising their own position and for combating socialistic errors."

Under head No. 6: The *Reformation and the Social Question:* "The fourth General Assembly of the Evangelical Alliance expresses its conviction that the mental and moral forces contained in the principle of the Reformation are sufficient for effecting that Reformation of Christian society which has become imperative, that in this way alone revolutionary socialism can be overcome." So in one of the latest meetings of the Evangelical-Social Congress at Berlin, consisting of all forms of Protestant thought in Germany, the celebrated ex-Court Chaplain Stoecker said that in the reconciliation of Individualism and Socialism lies the solution of the social question, and that the claims of Socialism for a greater development of its principle of *solidarity* in the present condition of society are an important factor of social evolution.

So far from taking up a position of unmitigated antagonism Protestant Churchmen everywhere have of late years endeavoured to establish points of contact with Socialism in a variety of ways, as the present writer has shewn in his work on "Christian Socialism". "Socialism is an idea," said one of the Church organs in Germany, as far back as 1875, "and in spite of some of its absurdities is a great reformatory idea, and against ideas, however perverse, the application of force cannot prevail." This was directed against attempts to put down socialism by authority. In its place, as is well known, a kind of "authoritative socialism"—*i.e.* State socialism, as in the case of legislation promoted by Prince Bismarck under the name of "Practical Christianity"—has gained ground in Germany, enjoying considerable favour in the highest places.

In a number of articles published in the clerical organ of this party in 1889—1890, commenting on a memorial drawn up by a special Committee of the *Inner Mission* on the duty of the Church in relation to the economic and social conflicts of the present day, the attitude of Modern Protestantism in relation to Socialism is clearly and amply defined. Here, both in text and comment we have the following principles broadly affirmed: that the Church is bound to concern herself with the whole of life here on earth and that social life must become interpenetrated with the leaven of the Gospel, that the religious and moral principles of Christianity must be indicated and applied to economics and the social life of the present day; so as to render existence less precarious, in the lower layers of society, to lessen the chasm which is widening between rich and poor and to insist on a greater regularity in the process of production; to combat materialism, gross or refined, in the higher and lower classes of society; for it is this which lies at the root of the self-seeking greed which is the characteristic of economic Liberalism, and it is this which dictates the demands of revolutionary Socialism, each man aiming at the highest degree of enjoyment in worldly goods. The Memorial proceeds to point out that Christ in His teaching and healing acts endeavoured to remove the causes of social evils in His day, and that modern Christianity, in a similar manner, must become again a moral power healing our social diseases arising from our social sins. In opposition to some current views as to man's position and destiny in the universe it says:—"The end of economic development we do not consider to consist in the equal and the highest satisfaction of earthly requirements for all, still less in the greatest possible acquisition of wealth irrespective of the welfare of individuals, but in such a reconstruction of industrial life as, without removing inequalities of possession and class differences, with their respective rights and duties and in accordance with the state of culture reached by each section of society, yet shall enable the lowest classes to attain to such a measure of material good as in the existing state of civilization shall secure them against economic distress and enable them to maintain and improve a moral state of existence." This would, it is assumed, prepare all for their higher future destiny hereafter. Further it is shewn that what is to be done has to be done not by formulating a social programme but by an appeal to Christian principle and the working out of Christian ideas. The only cure of mammonism is the Christian idea that man is a steward of the possessions entrusted to him; that in a Christian society all economic relations must be based on the principles of brotherly love; that money matters are subject to moral control; that as the family is the economic unit, the industrial relations of master and servants, employers and employed, ought to be as much as possible in the nature of the extension of the family life which would include the re-establishment of social relations between the capitalist and those under his employ.

The former is responsible for the bodily, moral and intellectual welfare of the latter. A lovely picture, as drawn by M. Flürscheim, is reproduced of Mynheer van Marken's establishment near Delft, where the master and mistress living in their own villa surrounded by the happy homes of their work people which are situated in the same park, represent, as it were, a happy family life. A description is given of the lodging-house, casino, library, distributive stores, schools, concert hall, shooting alley, and institutions of every kind for insurance, saving, and profit sharing, and a variety of societies for general intercourse. This is to shew how these principles are capable of practical application. Van Marken's yeast factory is the largest in Europe.

In England ideas like these have risen to the surface in the form of Christian Socialism. Ever since this name was given to the movement by F. D. Maurice in 1848, when he made the attempt of "Christianizing Socialism", it has been the aim of the Christian Socialists to reduce social abuses to a minimum, to introduce social reforms, to improve and increase the number of social institutions, so as to remove as far as possible the just causes of discontent with the existing social arrangements. In America there is a society of Christian Socialists having similar aims, basing their Christian Socialism on the Fatherhood of God, and the brotherhood of men, and "trying to carry it out in the spirit of Him Who was the First-born among many brethren." *

---

* The organ of this party is "*The Dawn*" from which we quote here an extract which appeared in the January number 1894, and indicates the drift or the movement:—

What is Christian Socialism? Christian is radically different from non-Christian Socialism; it differs *at the root*. In its economic *aim* it

It is with this aim—the same, so far, in Roman Catholic and Protestant countries—that Christian Socialists have formed themselves into a sacred phalanx to oppose anti-Christian tendencies in Socialistic agitation as carried on in the present day, whilst encouraging various forms of combination and co-operation for social ends on Christian

does not differ, but it believes that that aim can only be fulfilled by *starting from Christ*. It believes that God made man *one*, and made him for a kingdom *of joy and love*. But love must be free. Therefore God has not forced His kingdom upon man. Men have been left, by slow evolution and experience and history, to come to choose God's kingdom for themselves. Moses tried to institute it by law. Law failed and must fail to introduce love. Hence Christ came, God in man, to fulfil law in love, and lead men to the kingdom. Yet still was the Church He founded free to disobey. At first it worked for a kingdom of Heaven on earth. Then it went astray in asceticism and false spirituality resulting, like too much Christian science and mental science to-day, in the failure to understand the Incarnation which includes the divinity of matter as well as of spirit. But no portion of God's kingdom can be despised without penalty. Hence matter asserted itself, and shewed its power by re-acting on the Church and making her material and worldly, without spirit. The Protestant Reformation tried to escape this by individual spiritual return to God. But it did not yet see that the Incarnation means God in all life, matter as well as spirit, society as well as the individual. Hence it has only done a very partial, and in many ways misleading, work. Christian Socialists are therefore striving to bring the Church back to her primitive Catholic *unity and secularity*, and to establish God's kingdom on earth, through Christ, Who is the uniter, God in man, the head of the body of humanity. Socialism it considers an idle dream, occasioned, however, by Christian thought, but a dream that can be slowly, yet actually realized in Christian Socialism, through union with Christ, living from Him, and applying His law of brotherhood to society, politics, industry, productive and distributive.

In the January number for 1895 the *Dawn* refers to the progress of these ideas in the Episcopal Church of North America as evidenced by the utterances of bishops and others at the last Church Congress and expresses its intention to proceed to practically carrying out these ideas.

principles, with a view to conduct the socialist movement into safe channels.

The task is difficult, if not hopeless, since Socialism professes to be a new Gospel to supersede the old faith, and its leaders and many of its adherents tend to Atheism, Agnosticism, and other forms of unbelief. To say to such, that "the spirit and aspiration of Socialism has a Christian aspect", would seem to be little to the point. But what is meant here and in such-like phrases is this: That Socialism, as an ideal of society, as a protest against the selfish tendencies of individualism carried to excess, as an appeal to the social instincts of humanity, as an accentuation of its corporate life with corresponding duties of Christian men to each other, as an adumbration of a harmonized social order in which there would be room for the full and free exercise of social functions, as a combined effort to ensure the common welfare—Socialism, as a conception of a more perfect social state, where the maximum of social happiness and the minimum of social misery could be reached—Socialism in short, as a collective term, embracing every form of philanthropy and every scheme of social improvement, is not inconsistent with Christianity; but that, on the contrary, any attempt to realize its ideas must fail unless it has Christian principles for its basis and Christian love for its moving force.

This is the principle from which has sprung the recent revival of spiritual activity in the Christian world, what is called the new Christian Socialism, and the earnest discussion of social problems in every representative meeting of the Church of England. And in the same way we are assured by one who speaks with authority on the subject that never was there so strong an impetus among Nonconforming bodies to face the social problem in a Christian humanitarian spirit as in the present day. This is borne out by a perusal of the recent utterances at the Conference of Congregationalists and Baptists. All these signs of an awakening of Protestants to a higher sense of social duty, shew at least that Christianity is now, as in former ages, working through its ideas as a leaven in society, and in this manner Christianizing the Socialistic ideas of the age we live in. The teaching of the old Christian Socialists resolved itself into this one central doctrine, that association must re-combine the social units, each pursuing its own private interests; that co-operation in production and distribution must take the place of heartless and lawless competition; that concord among the workers and between themselves and the organisers of work must take the place of trade conflicts; that, in short, the confederation of labour must be brought about to replace the irregular, planless, and isolated pursuits of the individual without any sense of responsibility or care for the welfare of the community. "All this can be effected only," said the Christian Socialists, "by a radical change of opinion in the first instance." It is not by political and social changes that any permanent good can be effected, they maintained, against the political and economic theorisers of the day; what is wanted is a moral and religious, not a social and political, revolution. They appealed, in the first instance, to the moral conscience and placed convictions before actions. It is not your public measures and external machinery which will reform society, they said; your men must be reformed, and then the conduct of public affairs will help to bring about a happy consummation, begun in the effort of each moralised member of society. As long as people follow industrial pursuits from purely selfish motives, they will compete with one another, and combine against each other as if they were enemies. Let them learn to look not every one to his own things, but also to the things of others, and the antagonism which now frustrates the purpose of rivals will become an amicable endeavour to promote the welfare of all. In short, they revived the forgotten sentiment of Christian brotherhood; they were above all things determined to put to an end the fratricidal war of selfish interests, supposed then, and supposed even by some now, to be the prime motor of human progress. In this struggle for the best places each tried to reach the higher rung in the social ladder, unceremoniously knocking over the weaker competitor. It was a ladder which, like that seen by Jacob in his dream, rested on the earth, indeed, but its top did not touch Heaven. The Christian Socialists turned men's eyes to better things. They, too, encouraged men to rise; but to a higher sense of mutual obligation, and a nobler conception of combined effort for the common good. Not more material enjoyment for each one, but greater moral and mental development for all, they said, was the object to be aimed at.*

The programme of the New Christian Socialism, *i.e.* the objects of the Christian Social Union, which was founded at Oxford not many years ago, are thus formulated:—

(1) To claim for the Christian Law the ultimate authority to rule social practice.

(2) To study in common how to apply the moral truths

---

* See Tract on *The Christian Socialist Movement and Co-operation* by the writer published by the Educational Committee of the Co-operative Central Board.

and principles of Christianity to the social and economic difficulties of the present time.*

(3) To present Christ in practical life as the Living Master and King, the enemy of wrong and selfishness, the power of righteousness and love.

It is curious to notice, too, how even French Protestants are being drawn into the current of this new movement, which has for its ruling motive the desire of permeating society with the leaven of Christianity, of lifting up working humanity to a higher level morally and materially, of lessening the trials and privations of labour, of reclaiming the lowest layers of the social residuum, and of restoring social peace throughout the civilized world. Thus we see a gradual return to the Christian principle, lost sight of for a time, that men should be fellow-workers, not economic rivals or enemies. This is the view taken by the *Revue Socialiste* in commenting on a report of the General Assembly of the Protestant Association for the practical study of social questions in 1889; it sees in it a propitious sign of the times; for the main principles advocated by speakers at this Conference, it says, bear the stamp of real interest in the social aspirations of the masses, as they refer to the unjust distribution of riches and the legitimate complaints of the poor labourers as well as the urgent necessity of solving the social problem by means of private philanthropy and an appeal to State interference. Here, remarks the organ of French Socialism "our readers will be most astonished and gratified to find among a religious body, formerly *bourgeois* to the core, expressions of

---

* Some excellent leaflets are published by this Body to encourage the effective study of social subjects by its members and further fruitful discussion of social problems.

doctrines most gratifying to advanced Socialists ". In a previous number the same Review had referred with equal satisfaction to some social studies by M. Charles Secrétan, the Protestant Philosopher, indited in a similar spirit.

From this it would appear that, after all, the anti-Social character, encouraged, as M. Comte taught, by the industrial development in Protestant countries, has been considerably modified of late; that points of contact have been established between Protestantism and Socialism; that, as Professor Caird in his able work on the Social Philosophy of Comte has pointed out, there is another side to Protestantism which Comte in his abhorrence of its revolutionary or destructive side overlooked, namely the constructive power of Protestantism in arming the populace with reason and the power of using it, so as to work out the social destiny of Democracy in vindicating the right of all to work out their own social salvation and to do this by a return to the primitive forms of Christian belief and practice, based on the autonomy of the conscience. Nor is it in accordance with fact, as von Hartmann affirms in his pessimist criticism of Romanism and Protestantism alike, that it is on Protestant soil that irreligious Socialism flourishes most, whilst in Roman Catholic countries it is in danger of being submerged by what he calls Social Democratic Jesuitism. It is because the centres of Industry are to be found in Protestant countries that we meet here a fuller development of Socialism, not because they are Protestant in religion. It is in Roman Catholic countries, such as in France, Italy and Spain, that Socialism is most irreconcilable in its attitude towards religion and society. From the present attitude of all Protestant bodies towards Socialism, and from the manner in which their advances are met by Socialists of the better sort intellectually speaking, we should rather draw the hope that a *modus vivendi* will yet be established between the representatives of Social reform and those who follow in the footsteps of the early reformers. Of Luther it was said that he led the people as far as the Red Sea, the sea of blood shed in the Peasant Wars, but no further, that he stopped short, frightened by the horrors of the social insurrection. Social reformers among Protestants of the present day must avoid incurring the charge of half-heartedness in the present attempts to stem social discontents. If it be true that the revival of these Christian Social ideas is part of a "great awakening of the religious sense and a consequent quickening of the social conscience, which, perhaps, will in the long run be seen to constitute the principal glories of the nineteenth century", Protestantism must contribute its share to these triumphs. The successful attempts of the principal Protestant bodies in Germany, irrespective of differences of opinion, to unite for the common purpose of holding annually an Evangelical Social Congress to discuss social subjects, is a welcome earnest of good things to come, as mutual dissension has proved all along the principal source of weakness among Protestants in facing the social problem. An attempt at one time was even made to unite German Protestants and Catholics in the work of social reform. But until this effort is crowned with success each must work separately and as far as possible on parallel lines towards the same object, emulating one another without envy, each aiming at excellence without trying to excel each other.*

---

* Here the author may be permitted to re-affirm what he urged in a paper read at the Church Congress at Hull; that the suggestion of

We know that throughout the world's history discords, caused by human error or selfishness, have to be reconciled by the introduction of a higher power for good. Thus Christianity itself came first into the world as a regenerating principle and a moral force in society. Its mission is the same now.

"The comparison between our modern conditions of Society with those of the ancient world shortly before its dissolution," says Lange, the Historian of Materialism, "has often been made the subject of remark of late, and undoubtedly there are remarkable analogies which are patent to the observant eye. We, too, have a profuse increase of wealth, and we have a Proletariate; we, too, have a corruption of morals and religion; the present forms of government are endangered and there is a widely diffused and deeply rooted belief in a general revolution, as imminent. On the other hand our age possesses also powerful remedies, and if the storms of the transitional crisis will not go far beyond our present expectations, it is not likely that humanity will have to recommence its mental work as in the time of the Merovingians. One of the most important remedies is undoubtedly contained *in the ideas of Christianity*, the moral effect of which has

the Bishop of Derry, at a former Church Congress, for the creation of a chair of Sociology in the Universities for this purpose, should be forthwith acted upon, that it is desirable to appoint itinerant professors, serving several colleges and schools of divinity, or otherwise to provide for a course of lectures on social subjects to be delivered during the curriculum of theological students, or at its close. Also, that prize-essays for the encouragement of such studies under the direction of a central committee connected with the Church, might prove valuable. Two of the most valuable contributions to the subject are prize-essays written for the Christian Evidence Society at the Hague in 1874.

been as often underrated by some as it has been exaggerated by others."

In times past the ruling tendency in society was to benefit the few at the expense of the many, but now everything tends to shew that the tendency is to benefit the many at the expense of the few. It is accompanied by a change from Utilitarianism to Altruism, or a tendency to substitute for the moral principle of utility that of disinterestedness. In short, it is a tendency to make self-interest subordinate to the solidarity of interests of the whole human race. Its goal is the highest spiritual development of man, or Humanity, "unto the measure of the stature of the fulness of Christ". It is the more excellent way, though often missed by so-called Christians, who cannot divest themselves of false ideas of goodness and the highest good, mere heathenish survivals in our Christian civilization. The chief obstacle is still the carnal love of the world which idolizes wealth, power and success, and stands in the way of this final consummation, and it is the duty of Christian men to oppose this hindrance to real and spiritual progress.

"I confess," says J. S. Mill, "I am not charmed with the ideal of life held out by those who think that the normal state of human beings is that of struggling to get on; that the trampling, crushing, elbowing, and treading on each other's heels, which form the existing type of social life, are the most desirable lot of human kind, or anything but the disagreeable symptoms of one of the phases of industrial progress.... But the best state for human nature is that in which, while no one is poor, no one desires to be richer, nor has any reason to fear being thrust back by the efforts of others to push themselves forward." This is the ideal state of a political economist. Protestant divines, or Catholic for that matter, with the Book of the Prophet Isaiah and the Epistle of St. James before them should not be less strenuous in teaching and practising unworldliness. Are not a moderate sufficiency of means and quiet enjoyment more favourable to the growth of spiritual grace than our modern life at high pressure? Does not the highest effort of the inner life depend on the cultivation of a calm and contented disposition? Is not a constant state of conflict in competition with others unfavourable to growth in the passive virtues of Christianity and the development of certain benevolence? Is not our insatiable acquisitiveness in the midst of affluence as far removed as it can be from the ideal of that heavenly state where "they hunger no more, neither thirst any more"? Is not the restless race for wealth in the present day the worst preparation for the enjoyment of celestial peace?

Pleonexia, or greed, the unstilled appetite of accumulation of goods ending in satiety of pleasure, as the object of life, was reckoned among and condemned with the most obnoxious vices of society in the days of the Apostles; it is the most prominent feature of modern life. The followers of the Apostles and their flocks should never cease to raise their voice against it, and most strenuously to oppose it, both in teaching and living. In so doing they would most effectually rebut the charge of encouraging egoistical greed and avaricious self-seeking, justly or unjustly preferred against Protestantism.

SUMMARY AND CONCLUSION

WE have now passed through the various phases of modern thought and their correspondence with or opposition to the modes of socialistic thought in the present day; we have seen how at times the two currents are attracted towards and repelled from each other, and that upon the whole, as we should have expected from the nature of the case and before an examination of the facts and phenomena, Socialism must be regarded as a confluent or tributary of the general stream of contemporary thought and life rather than a counter-current to the intellectual movement of the present day.

We have seen how it falls in with the prevalent theories of those scientific teachers and their *soi-disant* followers, who accept the mechanical view of the Universe and with it a materialistic view of social evolution with its practical consequences. But we have also noticed signs of a turning of the tide, such as is observed among the recognized exponents of modern science, towards a more spiritual conception of the universe, or at least a scepticism more or less pronounced in the efficacy of monistic naturalism, as affording a full explanation of social existence or as an intellectual lever for raising and perfecting society. We have seen, too, how in its attitude towards the most important scientific theory of the age, Darwinism, Socialism is inconsistent with itself, hailing it as an ally at one moment and denouncing it as an enemy the next. For the struggle for existence and the principle of competition are one and the same, and in this effort of escaping from the dilemma not only Socialists, but scientific men like Huxley, or would-be social philosophers like Kidd, are guilty of the same inconsistency in their endeavour to reconcile their humanitarian yearnings with their scientific theory. Mr. Huxley refuses in morals the acceptance of the principle prevailing in the cosmic process which brings about the survival of the fittest, and Mr. Kidd does not seem to see that "social efficiency" which, he says, results from a rational pursuit of individual enterprise, would be sacrificed with the introduction of altruism on supra-natural grounds, forgetting apparently that selfishness is not the only natural instinct we possess.

These inconsistencies do honour to the heart of the Socialist, the scientist, and the social reformer, but they also show that the theory of natural selection in itself and by itself proves insufficient for the solution of the social problem.

Again, in dwelling on the ethics of socialism we observed the high standards of action upheld in its theory with human solidarity for its ideal and end. But we also noticed how, in the practical application of these principles and in its party manoeuvres, Socialism often falls below them, in which no doubt it fares no worse than other systems with greater spiritual pretensions, but which in the case of Socialism building up its moral system on the basis of fact, and on a purely material foundation, is less excusable. For whilst we do not expect human beings to reach Divine standards, or the nature of man to be raised to the full height of supernatural perfection, we have a right to expect those who acknowledge none but natural laws and sanctions to live up at least to their presumably less exalted and less exacting code of ethics.

We noticed that the fault of the system here lies in the absence of higher ideals and the weakness of moral momentum, in the absence of the spiritual ardour and enthusiasm imparted by religion, to bring about the promised social regeneration. We saw how as critics Socialists are pessimistic, whilst in the construction of their own scheme of social reconstruction they are optimistic overmuch, from which it is not unfair to conclude that there must be some fault in their analysis of the present social system and some error in their forecast of the society of the future; that in this respect again Socialism only reflects the oscillations of modern thought, now tending this way now that, according to passing modes of the *Zeitgeist*, and that the safe middle course lies in the hope of a scientific meliorism which steers clear between the two extremes; in other words that to avoid the disappointments which follow on exaggerated optimistic hopes, and the laming efforts of a weary and hopeless pessimism, we must look to social reform instead of to social revolution for a gradual though radical change of the existing social system; that we must set about to reform it on the principle of positive fact, avoiding the fictions and fallacies of a distorted pessimistic imagination and feverishly excited optimistic expectancy.

This led to the comparison of Positivism with Socialism as two rival social creeds in the present day. We saw that whilst both have much in common and an intellectual affinity exists, as Comte observed, between the aims of Socialism to establish the principle of solidarity as opposed

SUMMARY AND CONCLUSION

to egoism and the aims of Positivism to raise altruism or love of our neighbour into the leading principle of social action, yet serious diversities of aims and methods exist also, which prevent a fusion being effected between the two movements; that the aristocratic and hierarchical tendencies of Positivism and the democratic and equalitarian principles of Socialism are exclusive of one another, and that the slow progress of Comtism to win over the masses is a proof of this incompatibility between the two systems.

We next considered how far Socialism may be regarded as the friend or enemy of modern culture, and inquired how far the friends and representatives of culture are justified in their fear that modern Socialists, like the Vandals, if victorious would sweep away the last vestiges of modern civilization. A careful examination of the subject showed that on the whole this fear is unfounded; that culture which *has* survived the Vandals is not in danger of being swamped by Socialism, but that, on the contrary, even in the event of a socialist triumph, culture, literary, scientific, and artistic, would survive and prosper. At the same time we indicated the natural antagonism that exists between the men of action and the men of thought, and which accounts for the instinctive dislike and fear with which the conservative literary class regards the revolutionary innovator, and we drew the conclusion from this that culture as such is not capable of solving the social problem and satisfying the claims of Socialism; and also that whilst the plea of socialists for material betterment as the pre-requisite for improved mental culture is justified within limits it is none the less true that on the progress of culture—not only mental but chiefly moral—all round must be founded the hope of social improvement.

Lastly we considered the relation between modern Socialism and modern religious thought in its two principal manifestations, Roman Catholic and Protestant. It was pointed out what are the efforts made by Catholics to meet the demand for social reform and supply the need of social reorganization, the many points of contact where Romanism and Socialism meet, also where they are divergent in their aims and methods; but whilst willingly admitting the advances made by Romanism in winning over and organizing under its sway vast bodies of working-men not yet caught in the net of Socialism, (especially in mainly Protestant countries where both are arrayed against a common enemy, the *Bourgeoisie*,) we also noticed that in purely Roman Catholic communities the opposition between the claims of the Church and those of Labour have proved irreconcilable and the enmity between Romanism and Socialism is most virulent.

We proceeded in the last place to dwell on the relation of Protestantism, as a mode of religious thought, to Socialism, to consider how far the charge of diametrical opposition of their principles is justified, and to what extent it is true that capitalism, *laissez-faire*, and the faults of modern industry supposed to flow from them, are the direct outcome of the principles of the Reformation practically applied in Protestant countries. We endeavoured to show that the Renaissance, contemporary discoveries, the revival of natural science, and the adaptation of scientific discoveries to mechanical processes are partly responsible for this; and how, on the other hand, in all Protestant countries attempts at social reform and reforms in economic science, as well as the growth of philanthropic institutions to lessen and remove the effects of social pressure, are a

SUMMARY AND CONCLUSION 179

sign of an awakening of Protestant thought to the duty of remedying existing social evils. We next pointed out in a few counsels of perfection what is yet lacking in these efforts; and what remains now is to hope and wait and work for better things.

The current of human thought will not and cannot be retarded. Religious, philosophical and scientific thought in its direct and indirect influence on ethics, individual and social, cannot fail considerably to change the phases of society, though not always with the same speed nor in the same direction. Social forces ever at work will be propelled this way or that, according to prevailing changes in thought and intellectual development. Nor is ours the only age in which the human mind has been stirred in its deepest depths by changes in the actual world around us, and by reflection on the past, and an eager looking forward to coming changes in the future, and in turn has reacted on the course of events. It is possible in this transition state, nay, it is certain, that we exaggerate the importance of the epoch in which we live and its influence on the future fate of our race, as it is quite possible that we magnify unduly the greatness of the danger of the revolutionary changes through which we are passing or are likely to pass.

But to avoid as far as possible overrating our own importance, or being frightened by imaginary peril, we must try to see, as far as we can impartially and clearly, whither we are drifting and what are the intellectual and moral forces which are driving us onward. Only in so doing can we measure to some extent our strength and weakness in coping with the difficulties of the hour. It is only in the performance of our twofold duties of purifying the religious and moral conceptions of the thought of the present day and practically applying it to present day problems that we can hope to help forward the social movement of our race in its confused aims and generous aspirations, preparing the way for the evolution of the society of the future.

INDEX

A.

Adams, F. on Socialism 102, on Art 119.
Altruism in relation to Socialism 39.
American Christian Socialism 163.
Anarchism and Anarchists 3, 26, 53.
Arnold, Matthew, on relation of culture to Social Democracy 108—9.
Art in relation to Socialism 119 seq.
„ prospects of, in Socialist State 129.
Association as an economic principle 146, 159.

B.

Bax, E., Belfort 12, 109, 153.
Bebel, August, vii, 47, 60.
Beesley, Professor 56, 89.
Blanc, Louis, on Social Environment 49.
Bonar, James, on Social Philosophy 15.

Bourgeoisie and Bourgeois Egoism 7, 96.
Bourgeoisie and Catholic Socialism 132.
Brook Farm 114.

C.

Caird, Professor E., on Comtism and its Social bearings 94.
Capital and Protestantism 153.
Capitalism 51, 135, 139.
Catholic movement in relation to Socialism 132.
Christianity and Socialism 12, 16, 171.
Christian Philanthropy 36, 157.
Christian Socialists, Old and New 163—9.
Claperton, Jane Hume, on Social amelioration 73—4.
Competition 48.
Comte's view of Society and Social improvement 78, 97.
Congreve, Dr. 87, 98.
Crozier, on Progress 67.
Culture and Socialism 102 seq.

D.

Darwinism and Socialism 17, 23, 92, 174.
Délon, Dr., on relation of Pessimism to Socialism 60, 96.
Déville, on Science in connection with Socialism 25.

E.

Economic Materialism 4 seq.
Egoism and Individualism 154—5.
Eliot, George, on Social meliorism 39.
English Socialism in Novels 112—13.
Ethical Optimism 72.
Equality 45, 67.
Expropriation 11, 19.

F.

Fatalities of Nature and "Social Predestination" 5.
French Socialist Novels 115.
Force, Moral and physical, used by Socialism 53.
Frohme, on Social duty 46.

G.

Gautier, E., on le Darwinisme Social 19.
George, Henry, 11, 46, 73.
Graham, Professor on Socialism and Science 28.

H.

Harrison, Frederic 79, 85, 88, 96—8.
Haeckel, E., 24, 42.
Hartmann, E. von 65, 75, 169.
Hitze, on Social Economics from R. Catholic standpoint 138.
Huxley, Professor 59, 175.

I.

Ideals, Social and literary, etc. 117—18, 128.
Individualism and Socialism, 133—5, 141—3, 153.
Ingram, Professor T. K., 91.

J.

Jaurés, J., 47.

K.

Kidd, Benjamin, 15, 30, 34, 77, 95.

L.

Labour, short hours of 44.
Labour, Church 15.
Lafargue, on Socialism and Darwinism 25, 42.
Laissez-faire, laissez aller 41, 50, 132.
Land Question from Socialist standpoint 51.
Lassalle on Culture and Socialism 103.
Le Play, on Religion in relation to the Social Question 152.

"Letters from Nowhere" 121.
Leo XIII, Pope, on the Social Problem 130, 152.
Levi, Leone, on Economic progress 168.
Literature in relation to Socialism 106—116.
"Looking backwards" 102, 111.

M.

Mackenzie, J. S., 15.
Maine, Sir H. Sumner 9.
Malon, Bénoit, 44—5, 58, 72.
Mallock, W. H., on Socialism in relation to Art 121.
Materialism and Socialism 4, 14, 18, 33, 40, 59, 97.
Meliorism, Social and Scientific 35, 73—4.
Milieu, *i.e.* Environment in its effects socially 27, 40, 49.
Mill's socialism 45.
Molinari, G. de, on Economic Individualism and Competition 40.
Monism in its philosophical bearings on Socialism 32 seq.
Morals of Socialism 8, 38 seq.
Morris, William 119, 122, 125.
Mun, le Comte de, on Catholic Socialism 136, 148.

N.

Natural Revival and Socialistic Aims 18.
Novels, Socialist 110 seq.

O.

Optimism 67.

P.

Pessimism and Socialism 61 seq. 176.
Philosophy of Socialism 1 seq.
Pleonexia, on passion of accumulation 46, 173.
Plutocracy 106.
Poetry, Socialist 123, 128.
Political Economy of Romanist writers 138.
Political hypocrisy of Socialists 54.
Positivism in relation to Socialism 78 seq. 177.
Potier, Eugène, Socialist poems 126.
Protestantism and Socialism 135, 149, 153, 178 seq.
Proudhon 135. On Property 145
Psychic Method of Social Evolution 35.

R.

Ratzinger, R., Catholic Economics 138.
Reformation and Renaissance and Capitalism 156—7.
Religion and Social Democracy 12, 39, 57, 153.
Religion of Humanity and Socialism 95.
Resolutions of Evangelical Social Congress 153, 160, 170.

Revolution and Catholic Reaction 134.
Romanism and Socialism 130, seq. 178.

S.

Salt, H. S., on Literature in relation to Socialism 105.
Science and Socialism 28—9, 35, 67.
Shairp, on Culture 104.
Scheel, von, 1, 12.
Scherer, E., 100.
Schmidt, O., 23.
Schopenhauer, A., 65.
Schulze-Gävernitz 93.
Social Democracy and Christianity 145.
Social Future of working-classes 89.
Social Evolution and Revolution 6, 77, 99.
Socialist Novels 110 seq.
Sociocracy 84.
Sociology 80, 92.
Solidarity, the end of Social Development 96—7.
State-Socialism 144—6, 149, 158.
Statistics of Social progress 69.
Sumner, Professor, on Ethics of Economics 55.

T.

Toynbee, Arnold, 94.
Tourgenieff, on Nihilists 112.
Trades-unionism 90.
Tchernichewski's Nihilist Novel 111.

U.

Utopia Brook Farm in U. S. 114.

V.

Van Marken's practical Scheme of Social amelioration 163.
Vogelsang, Baron von, on State-Socialism in Austria 145.

W.

Wages, Iron law of 140.
Walster, Otto's socialist novels 114.
Working-man's Philosophy 9.

Z.

Zola's novels read by Socialists 115.